HANGING *on to* HoPE

Advance Praise for
HANGING *on to* HoPE

"Do you long to believe that God is real? Do you want to believe that He cares for your every need? Do you desire to believe in miracles again? These daily devotionals will address these questions no matter where you are in your life today. Your faith will be encouraged, challenged, and renewed by Diane's down-to-earth true stories. The scriptural references, inspired poems, and heartfelt prayers will bless and draw you nearer to God. During those quiet moments with God, you will come to realize that no matter what you go through, God will never leave you and He is your HOPE."

—Erin Timberlake

"Thanks to Diane, the author of *Hanging on to Hope*, for sharing many chapters of her life with us. Life is one of the greatest classrooms for discovering God and His Presence. As a living epistle she has written to many with the Spirit of The Living God, touching the tablets of human hearts. Her personal experiences, testimonies, and revelations will provide Hope for many."

—Pastor James Henson

HANGING on to HOPE

*Clinging to
Christ in
the Midst of
the Mess*

DIANE MEYER

NASHVILLE

NEW YORK • LONDON • MELBOURNE • VANCOUVER

HANGING *on to* HoPE

Clinging to Christ in the Midst of the Mess

© 2022 DIANE MEYER

Published in New York, New York, by Morgan James Publishing. Morgan James is a trademark of Morgan James, LLC. www.MorganJamesPublishing.com

Proudly distributed by Ingram Publisher Services.

Scripture quotations marked (NASB) taken from the (NASB®) New American Standard Bible®, Copyright © 1960, 1971, 1977 by The Lockman Foundation. Used by permission. All rights reserved.

Scripture quotations marked (NLT) are taken from the Holy Bible, New Living Translation, copyright ©1996, 2004, 2015 by Tyndale House Foundation. Used by permission of Tyndale House Publishers, Carol Stream, Illinois 60188. All rights reserved.

Scripture quotations marked (KJV) from The Authorized (King James) Version. Rights in the Authorized Version in the United Kingdom are vested in the Crown. Reproduced by permission of the Crown's patentee, Cambridge University Press.

Scripture marked (NKJV) taken from the New King James Version®. Copyright © 1982 by Thomas Nelson. Used by permission. All rights reserved.

Scripture quotations marked (NIV) are taken from the Holy Bible, New International Version®, NIV®. Copyright © 1973, 1978, 1984, 2011 by Biblica, Inc.™ Used by permission of Zondervan. All rights reserved worldwide. The "NIV" and "New International Version" are trademarks registered in the United States Patent and Trademark Office by Biblica, Inc.™

Scripture quotations marked (ESV) are from The ESV® Bible (The Holy Bible, English Standard Version®), copyright © 2001 by Crossway, a publishing ministry of Good News Publishers. Used by permission. All rights reserved.

Scripture marked (NCV) taken from the New Century Version®. Copyright © 2005 by Thomas Nelson. Used by permission. All rights reserved.

Scripture marked (BSB) taken from The Holy Bible, Berean Study Bible, BSB

Copyright ©2016, 2020 by Bible Hub

Used by Permission. All Rights Reserved Worldwide.

Morgan James BOGO™

A **FREE** ebook edition is available for you or a friend with the purchase of this print book.

CLEARLY SIGN YOUR NAME ABOVE

Instructions to claim your free ebook edition:
1. Visit MorganJamesBOGO.com
2. Sign your name CLEARLY in the space above
3. Complete the form and submit a photo of this entire page
4. You or your friend can download the ebook to your preferred device

ISBN 978-1-63195-761-1 paperback
ISBN 978-1-63195-762-8 ebook
Library of Congress Control Number: 2021917563

Cover Design by:
Rachel Lopez
www.r2cdesign.com

Morgan James PUBLISHING Builds with... **Habitat for Humanity** Peninsula and Greater Williamsburg

Morgan James is a proud partner of Habitat for Humanity Peninsula and Greater Williamsburg. Partners in building since 2006.

Get involved today! Visit MorganJamesPublishing.com/giving-back

This book is for my wonderful husband, Jeff. He believed in me; he edited, typed, and read; and he was my great helpmate. Without him, this book would not have been possible. Thank you, sweetheart.

To my children, Joie and Jenna. As you read these devotionals, may you come to know your mother's heart for God and the awesomeness of the Lord I serve. And to Ryder Joseph, my grandson. You bring me so much joy. You are a blessing to me, and I love you with all my heart!

To the residents and employees of Lifehouse Christian Maternity Home. I love you because you are miraculous ladies who minister to me.

To Joan Smith, the original founder of Lifehouse, who had the vision of the Christian Maternity Home in the first place. I give you my love, thanks, and admiration. Thanks for the encouragement along the way, dear friend.

TABLE OF CONTENTS

ACKNOWLEDGMENTS

I want to acknowledge and thank Meredith Jones of Studio 199 for being my wonderful web designer, photographer, and friend. She was patient in teaching me about blogging, recording videos, and posting on YouTube.

I acknowledge Brenda Kilgour, who edited my manuscript and offered her comments, Aubrey Kosa as final editor, and Morgan James Publishing.

INTRODUCTION

"The Spirit of the Lord God is upon me, because the Lord has anointed me to bring good news to the afflicted, He has sent me to bind up the broken hearted, to proclaim liberty to captives, and freedom to prisoners; to proclaim the favorable year of the Lord, and the day of vengeance of our God; to comfort all who mourn, to grant those who mourn in Zion, giving them a garland instead of ashes, the oil of gladness instead of mourning, the mantle of praise instead of a spirit of fainting. So they will be called oaks of righteousness, the planting of the Lord, that he may be glorified."

—Isaiah 61:1–3 (NASB)

You may ask yourself why I would write this devotional and what qualifies me to do so. For me, the answer is as simple as the air that I breathe. Only God and his overcoming Holy Spirit have sustained me through molestation, miscarriage, a stillborn baby girl, death, divorce, family members with addictions, sickness, heartache that goes clear to the bones, disappointment, broken dreams, and plentiful mourning.

People have forsaken me, but God never, ever has. He has brought me through these trials, afflictions, and adversities by changing and sustaining me. His spirit has poured his anointing on me that I may minister to these same needs in you. It is when the vessel that holds the oil is broken that the anointing is released. Friends, I have been broken on numerous occasions, in the past and in the present. I have felt practically every mental, physical, and emotional pain known to man.

I have finally chosen to walk into the destiny for which God has called me. That destiny is to minister to you, to encourage you, to hold your hand through brokenness, and to cry with you—just as my "ever present help in time of trouble" has done for me. Jesus is the greatest teacher, and my relationship with Him has qualified me to do unto you as He has done unto me. Every page of this book has come forth through God's anointing after my brokenness. I pray that you will feel God's heart and hands reach out to you and that the Prince of Peace will bring peace into your situation and heart right now.

GOD, I DON'T UNDERSTAND!

"I can do all things through Christ who gives me strength."
—Philippians 4:18 (NKJV)

"Please God, no. I don't understand. Just make it go quickly."

I was five months pregnant, and my gynecologist had just told me that my baby had died in my uterus. This was my third pregnancy, and I still had no baby. The other two pregnancies had ended in miscarriage, one at three months and the other at six weeks. I had finally made it into the second trimester and was jubilant and filled with hope. We had just finished the nursery because we were finally going to have our baby.

Just the day before, I had gone to my monthly checkup with Dr. Hyman. He was very concerned because he couldn't get a heartbeat. He had the nurse take me into another room to do an ultrasound and still saw no movement or heartbeat. He asked me if my husband was with me. My husband had just gotten off work and was sitting in the car waiting for me to finish with my appointment. Dr. Hyman told me to go get him because he needed to talk to us. I knew the situation was serious, but I had no idea about the trial that lay ahead of us.

Dr. Hyman explained that there was no movement or heartbeat. This meant that our baby had died. He told us to go home and return to the hospital the next morning. Another ultrasound would be performed. If no life was found, appropriate measures would be taken at that time.

We were in shock for the next twenty-four hours. We prayed and called everybody that we knew to pray for us. Needless to say, we slept very little. The next morning, I packed a suitcase and went to the hospital.

After the doctor's diagnosis had been confirmed, Dr. Hyman explained that he would have to induce labor to prevent infection and further complications. Before the labor began, though, I was to receive medication for nausea, fever, vomiting, and high blood pressure because these were side effects that accompanied the medication that would put me into labor. That was when I uttered the prayer, "Please God. I don't understand. Just make it go quickly."

I had always heard that God doesn't promise you a life without trials, but He does promise that He will go through the trials with you. Even though I didn't understand why I had to endure this difficult trial, I knew that God was with me. I had felt His presence since I was a child. I knew that I could do this with His help, but it is not the road that I would have chosen.

The nausea, diarrhea, vomiting, fever, and high blood pressure hit me suddenly and with the force of a tornado. I was so sick and weak that I couldn't tell them which end of me needed the bedpan. The next thing I knew, I was telling myself, "Don't push, Diane. Don't push."

The nurse checked my labor progress and told them to call Dr. Armstrong and get me to labor and delivery! Dr. Armstrong was on call that day. The nurses gave me a shot of morphine on the way to the delivery room because my doctors didn't want the pain to dissuade me from getting pregnant again. The bright lights in the delivery room were the last thing I remembered before telling them that I needed to push. My eyes grew heavy and closed.

When I awoke, I was in my room at Norton's Hospital. A nurse came in and talked to me about what had happened. She asked if there was anything that I needed and told me that she would be with me during the night shift. I cannot explain what happened or how she made me feel the way she did, but I can tell you that each time she entered the room, I felt a heavenly peace and warmth. She had a beautiful, comforting smile. I knew that she cared about me and that I was not alone. I felt as if an angel was present with me to bring comfort and hope. I never saw her again but was eternally thankful for the part she played in my delivery and mourning of Bethany Nicole, my precious baby girl.

I have no doubt that God was with me feeling my pain when I knew that the labor I was to endure would only bring forth a dead baby. Why? I knew what the Bible said about my situation. *I can do all things through Christ who gives me strength.* This was one of the many trials in which God proved his faithfulness to me.

Are you going through something right now that you think is too hard? If so, grab on to this promise. Tell yourself, the devil, and whoever else needs to hear these words that you can do all things because Christ will give you the strength.

> *Dear God,*
>
> *I don't understand why I must endure this situation, but I do know that you are with me. It seems impossible to me, but I know that it is not too big for you. Help me, God. Hold my hand as a Daddy holds the hand of their little one just beginning to walk. Daddy, don't let me fall. Don't let go. Go with me through the pain, through the difficulty, and through the trial! I trust you, Lord. Amen.*

THE DREAM

"Now faith is being sure of what we hope for and certain of what we do not see."
—Hebrews 11:1 (NIV)

Holding a precious baby in my arms, my own child, was my heart's desire. Since I had already endured three unsuccessful tries at pregnancy, I was beginning to question whether it would ever happen for me. I began to search the scriptures and to stand on the promises of God. I joined a women's Bible study and asked them to join me in praying for a child. I had read and believed all that pertained to the promise of children.

One week, three nights in a row, I dreamed of a baby. In the first dream, I was picking up the baby from the crib. In the second dream, I was rocking and looking down at the baby. In the third dream, I was changing the diaper, and it was a little boy. It was always the same baby—in my arms, in my prepared nursery, in my home.

I walked over to my neighbor, Dakota's, house, who was also in my Bible Study. I shared the dreams with her. She asked me what the baby looked like, and I told her that he had brown hair, tanned skin, and blue eyes. Dakota began to exclaim that she, too, had dreamed of the same baby that week. We agreed that it must be the child that God was going to give me.

Not long after that, I found out that I was pregnant. This is when I found out what having faith really meant because I had to endure the same trials that I had in my previous three pregnancies. I did all that I could to prevent miscarriage. I took no medication, not even for headaches. I drank no caffeine. I did not lift heavy objects, and I even quit my job so that I could fully concentrate on a healthy pregnancy.

In each of my other pregnancies, I had nausea and vomiting all day long for several months. I started out the fourth pregnancy the same way. I had been learning how we need to stand on the word of God and decided to do that in this case also. One morning, I was standing over the commode vomiting when the Lord quickened this in my heart. I got my Bible and literally stood on it as I was vomiting. I quoted whatever scriptures came into my mind. I finally believed that God could help me through the nausea and vomiting.

"By his stripes, I am healed. Beloved, I wish above all things that thou mayest prosper and be in good health even as thy soul prospers. Ask and it shall be given unto you. With men it is impossible, but not with God, for with God, all things are possible."
3 John 1:2 (KJV)

The morning—or in my case, all day—sickness lasted less than in my previous pregnancies.

Later, I began spotting, at the same point I had in my other pregnancies.

Once again, I had to hang on to faith in God and His word. Then, at about five months into my pregnancy, my baby quit moving. For an entire week, I didn't feel any movement. That was followed by my breasts leaking.

It was at five months into my third pregnancy, when I had these exact same symptoms, that the doctor said Bethany had died. Needless to say, I was concerned. The enemy of my soul was trying to make me afraid. The only thing that kept me going was the image of that baby boy I had seen in my dreams and the scriptures I had been studying. This kept my faith and hope alive.

When I waited in the doctor's office for my five-month checkup, I was yearning to hear my baby's heartbeat. I had to wait three hours because Dr. Hyman was called into three deliveries, but I was not going home until I saw him. Finally, when he entered and asked me how I was doing, I said, "Fine, I hope."

He put his clipboard down on my pregnant, draped tummy and began to talk to me. He said, "Honey, you have to have faith."

I had heard that he was a Christian, but this was the first time he had shared his faith with me. He went on to tell me that God was the one who delivered the babies and he was just the hands used by God to do so. He let me hear the heartbeat and pronounced me healthy and on schedule. What a joy it was!

I shared my dreams with him, and he told me to claim that little boy. Four months later when I went into labor, Dr. Hyman was on call for my delivery. I went into the hospital not knowing for sure if I was in labor. I was still in my first stage of breathing when they informed me that I was in transition. God's presence was so real that I scarcely felt the pain. I had no medication. I didn't scream or yell like the labor and delivery coach said I might do. I didn't get sick. The labor progressed so quickly that the next thing I knew, I was telling myself, "Don't push, Diane. Don't push." The nurse checked my progress and said to get me to delivery pronto!

Dr. Hymen barely got there in time, but when he came into the room, he asked, "What are you supposed to have?"

I replied, "A boy!"

After a few pushes, Dr. Hyman said, "Hallelujah, here's your son!"

It was the same baby boy from my dreams. I know that God gave me those dreams so that I could endure the trials and tests of my pregnancy and have faith in God for the promise of my son, Joie. On May 14, 1981, I gave birth to a beautiful, brown-haired, blue-eyed, precious baby boy!

If you are going through a trial right now, have faith in God. God showed me that many positive people have faith in their own faith, not faith in God. Our own faith may fail us, but God will never fail us. I hope the poem that God provided to encourage me also encourages you today.

FAITH IN GOD

Sometimes I get discouraged when things start falling apart.
The storm begins to rage and torment my troubled heart.
When I start looking at my problems instead of at my Lord,
I become doubtful and impatient, and fear becomes my reward.

You see, it's really simple. Faith in God is the key.
If in all things we can trust him, with him,
we'll spend eternity.
Since he'll never leave or forsake us
and works all things for our best,
Don't fear the clouds and storms of life.
Have faith in God, and in him rest!

THANK GOD IN THE MIDST OF THIS?

"Always giving thanks for all things in the name of our Lord Jesus Christ to God, even the Father."
—Ephesians 5:20 (NASB)

N o, it can't be. This had to be a bad dream. God would not allow this to happen to them again.

In my shock, these were the thoughts I had as I received the news of my niece, baby Jessica's, death. I had just seen her at the hospital the day before and had been told she would be coming home this evening. Instead, my husband met me as I was coming out the door of one of my Avon customers with this grave, shocking news.

Just a few years before, James and Lea had buried their eight-month-old son, Clint Matthew. He died of meningitis within

11

twenty-four hours of its onset. At the time, my brother was not saved, but through the loss off his son had acknowledged his need of a savior. In the months following the death of their precious, always smiling, little guy with a cherubic face, James gave his life to the Lord on May 4, 1980.

They had four-year-old Jason, Clint's older brother, and then God blessed them with Jessica Lane four years later. Jessica was born with a heart defect that would need to be repaired when she was old enough for the surgery. One Sunday morning before church, Jessica struggled to breathe. She was taken to the emergency room at the local hospital, and they said that she had aspirated on her saliva. James and Lea knew that was not right, so they took her to a hospital that specialized in pediatric medicine.

The doctors ran all kinds of tests to see whether she had a heart attack or whether her condition had worsened. They found some fluid in her lungs but found nothing else significant enough to have caused her breathing struggles. The plans were to release her on Monday evening until the nurses and doctors had witnessed for themselves her difficulty breathing. James and his pastor came to my parents' home sometime later. James said he had some news that he had to tell us. He didn't want it to go any further than the immediate family. There was an investigation into Jessica's death. When the morphine was administered, an error was made. She was given ten times the dosage that she needed. Immediately, her eyes rolled back into her head, and she was gone.

The verse does not say to thank God for all things, but to give him *thanks in all things*. James and Lea buried their second little one with the media following them everywhere because this error had made national television. Jessica's visitation had lines formed out the door of the funeral home. I stood by the casket and watched my sister-in-law laugh with joy and praise God for allowing them to talk about the love of God to the multitude of people who were coming to the funeral home. God comforted them. God carried them during this great time of grief.

You may be going through a trial right now in which you are convinced that *giving thanks in all things* is impossible. I can assure you that *when you are weak, God is strong.* I have seen this firsthand, in the most horrible of circumstances. I saw my brother and sister-in-law praise God during the funeral of their little Jessica, who was only sixteen months old. I saw the beauty that came out of their ashes. I saw this verse work firsthand, so it is possible.

Dear God,

You know exactly what I am going through and what I need. Even if I don't feel like it, I choose to praise and thank you for being here for me. I thank you for giving me peace, comfort, and help. I thank you for turning my mourning into dancing. I thank you for having all the answers to my needs. I simply ask you to be the lifter of my head and healer of my soul and to help me to do all things through your supernatural strength. Amen.

GOD'S PEACE

Thank you, Lord, for giving me peace
through trying times such as these.
To you, oh Lord, I surrender all
as I listen to your gentle call.
Even though I know not why,
and many times have begun to cry,
You, my friend, have dried my tears.
You, my God, have calmed my fears.
Thank you, Savior, for holding my hand
as I journey to your promised land.

CHILDLIKE FAITH

"And a little child shall lead them."
—Isaiah 11:6 (NASB)

While other kids my age complained about going to church, my greatest dream was to sit in church with my parents one day. I asked God to help them quit drinking, cussing, and smoking. I was too young to realize that what they needed was to receive salvation and let God change those things.

At Jessica's funeral, a man who came to pay his respects to my brother asked James, "Who is that man?" as he pointed to my dad. James told him it was his father and inquired why he asked. He said that my dad had darkness all over him.

When James got a break, he asked Dad to accompany him to the office. James asked Dad if he was ready to be saved. Dad said that he was, so my brother led him in the sinner's prayer at his daughter's funeral. What a miracle! This happened during a time of grief in a funeral home. This was the answer to many prayers prayed over the years by a little child.

Our little Jessica had gone to be with Jesus but had paved the way for many miracles when she left us. James prayed with the nurse who had followed the doctor's orders and administered the lethal dose of morphine to Jessica. She accepted Christ in the hospital. He led my dad to the Lord in the funeral home. James surrendered his life to answer a call of God to go into ministry. He talked about forgiveness on national television, which got the attention of *The 700 Club*. He and Lea were asked to share their testimony of forgiveness on one of *The 700 Club* episodes. People all over the world were touched by Jessica's story and the reaction of her parents to the error that had taken their baby girl's life. A little child led many to the Lord and is still doing so today.

James and Lea now pastor a church that is located on the same land that used to contain a gas station. That gas station had illegal gambling and sold whiskey in a back room. Our dad used to frequent that gas station and take advantage of its illegal benefits. Now this is a filling station of a different kind! How good is God!

Both of my parents were baptized within months of Jessica's death. I was granted my prayers to sit in church with them. My dad and mom were changed by the Lord and were even better parents in their later years. They were even better grandparents, and most of the grandchildren do not even have a memory or knowledge of their "before Christ" lives.

As a child, I prayed for my mom, dad, and brother. Once again, a little child had touched the heart of God. Not only did he answer a small child's prayers, but he made something more beautiful than even I had desired. My brother is an awesome pastor. His wife is an anointed music minister, and their son, Jason, is a wonderful youth pastor. Both of my parents have joined Clint, Jessica, Bethany Nicole, and other grandchildren. We shall see them all again one day.

No matter how messed up or painful your life is right now, God can and will make something beautiful of it. He has done it before and can do it again. Just pray this with me.

Dear God,

I surrender my heart, the hurting heart of a little child, into your hands. God, make something beautiful come out of this pain. Touch me and all those involved in this situation. I come to you as a little child and cry, "Daddy, help me. Hold me. Love me. Speak truths into this situation. Move the mountains of fear, unbelief, and discouragement so that I can receive your miracle for me today." Amen.

MUSTARD SEED FAITH

"If you have faith as a mustard seed, you shall say to this mountain, move from here to there, and it shall move; and nothing shall be impossible to you."
—Matthew 17:20 (NASB)

When I was a child, I did not have the privilege of attending church. God did draw me in, though. I remember going to doctor's appointments and enthusiastically reading the Bible stories for children. It was there that I first learned about a God who performed miracles. I read about Jesus healing the centurion's daughter and how God made the flour and oil last for the widow and her son. I learned about a God who cares and who is big enough to heal.

When I was almost seven, my second niece, Sherri, was born with a hole in her heart. It was serious enough that specialists were needed to treat her. She was protected from exposure to illness, wasn't allowed to be held by many, and was going to have open-heart surgery around the age of five. I remember my mother and my sisters talking about her condition with much concern and anxiety, so I decided to pray for her every night as I said my prayers. After all, God could heal. I read it in the children's Bible stories.

A few years later, when a cousin began picking me up and taking me to Sunday School and church services, I always raised my hand during prayer requests and asked that God would heal Sherri. I had the faith of a little child that God teaches about in the Bible.

After Sherri turned five, she was scheduled for a heart catheterization to see the extent of her damage in order to prepare her for surgery. I accompanied my anxious sister that day. It was a very somber mood, and I was only around twelve or thirteen years old. We were told that the hole in her heart was no longer there. It truly was a miracle because we had been told that the hole would only grow larger and would never close on its own.

You see, God had plans for Sherri. She had been told that she could never play sports like a normal child; however, she went on to be a volleyball, track, and basketball star. Now, over thirty years later, she still holds track records at North Harrison High School. Sherri went on to be the salutatorian of her class, win scholarships, get a bachelor's degree in nursing, marry a doctor, and have two sons. This was to be the first of many miracles that I witnessed God perform. Sherri's miracle was the catalyst of my belief in an awesome God that could and would answer prayer.

Are you in need of a miracle? Do you have a mustard seed of faith? Did you know that a mustard seed is the smallest of seeds? My friend, pray with me.

Dear God,

You know that I need a miracle. (Be specific and tell him what you need.) Your word says that we are to come to you with the faith of a little child and ask, believing that we will receive. Jesus, I am asking you for this miracle today. I will trust you to answer my prayer, even if it takes a while, even if it doesn't look like the answer is on its way. Today I know that you have begun to work on moving this mountain in my life. I trust you. I know that you are able, and I thank you, dear God. Amen.

JESUS, HELP!

"The righteous cry and the Lord hears, and delivers them out of all their troubles."
—Psalms 34: 17 (NASB)

I have always heard that Jesus has gone through anything that we have faced, but when I went through divorce, I asked God about this. How could he know the pain of the severe rejection of divorce since he had never married?

I was driving down the road crying because I loved my husband so much, and he had just told me that he didn't love me anymore and didn't know if he ever had. This was my high school sweetheart, the man for whom I had saved my virginity and pledged my love forever. I longed to hold him and love him, but he didn't want anything to do with me.

I felt such rejection. That's when the still, small voice spoke to me, "I long to love my children every day, but many want nothing to do with me. They don't love me and won't let me love them."

Knowing the pain I had felt from one man showed me how much pain the Lord had felt from so many. That pain and yearning of our rejected love was multiplied many times over. Wow! God really does understand what I am going through.

I was left with a five-month-old baby girl and an almost four-year-old son to raise on my own. I had no job. My car had broken down. I had no money to fix my car and felt as if I had nobody to turn to for help. After all, I was too old to run to my parents. After the kids were finally asleep, I felt trapped, alone, scared, and confused as I laid on my bed that night.

I began to weep and to pray for help, guidance, and understanding. That is when I decided to open my Bible for some comfort. It fell open to the thirty-fourth chapter of Psalms. This is what I read that night:

> *"The righteous cry, and the Lord heareth, and delivereth them out of all their troubles. The Lord is nigh unto them that are of a broken heart; and saveth such as be of a contrite spirit. Many are the afflictions of the righteous; but the Lord delivereth him out of them all. He keepeth all his bones: not one of them is broken. Evil shall slay the wicked: and they that hate the righteous shall be desolate. The Lord redeemeth the soul of his servants: and none of them that trust in him shall be desolate."*
> —*Psalms 34:17–22 (KJV)*

The next day, friends came to pray with me. As the two Christian friends were leaving, one of them handed me an envelope. He said that God had put it on his heart to give this to me. After he left, I opened the envelope and discovered that it was the exact amount of money that I needed to fix my car. Wow!

Later, when I shared this testimony with a friend who was going through the same thing, I made a fresh discovery. I told her that night as I laid on my bed crying that the word cry was in italics. This was God's way of showing me that he was with me and knew about all the details of my life. I opened my Bible to show her, and the word was not in italics. This was even more amazing to me. That night, long ago, when I needed to hear from God most, he had put the word in italics just for me. His word is living! It is powerful! It is personal! Do you have a heartache or a need right now? Pray the following poem that God gave to me.

I NEED YOU

Oh, dear Lord, I need you, more than ever before.
Here I come before you, knocking loudly at your door.
Take your arms and hold me, God. I need you, oh so much.
I desire your love and peace, the gentleness of your touch.
God, you alone know what I am feeling.
Begin in me an inner healing.
Lord, it is time for me to let go
Of all the memories that hurt me so.

DO YOU HEAR ME, GOD?

"Hear my cry, oh God. Attend unto my prayer. From the ends of the earth, will I cry unto thee. When my heart is overwhelmed, lead me to that rock that is higher than I. For thou has been a shelter for me and a strong tower from the enemy."

—Psalms 61:1–3 (KJV)

T he morning news warned of storms coming and issued tornado watches with a likelihood of damaging winds. I looked outside and saw the dark, black clouds looming and moving fast. This reminded me of my life in that moment— and of many times past. These are times when so many trials are looming overhead that I feel overwhelmed, weak, and unable to think or prioritize. Ever been there? If you have been a Christian for very long, I am sure that you have because that is exactly how the devil wants you to feel. He wants you to give up hope.

One such day for me was right after my divorce. I had heard mice, which I hate, in my bedroom. My ex-husband had picked up my bed, as agreed upon, but had taken my pillows as well. After spending the night on the couch, I started the day by taking care of my children. Jenna was crawling and had found the mouse trap in my closet with her little fingers. She cried and cried, and I felt like a failure as a mother because I had forgotten about the trap. The day continued to worsen because I had not yet found anybody to put up the new waterbed that I had purchased.

I was headed to take the kids to my mom's so that I could deliver Avon. It was almost dark, so I didn't see the telephone pole that had fallen off a truck just minutes before on this little country road. It had fallen perpendicular with the road so that it was impossible to detect until I came upon it. I had nobody to come and pick up the kids and me when my little Ford Escort was towed. I no longer had a husband who took care of things for me. This wasn't death, but it was overwhelming.

Then I remembered the above scripture about being overwhelmed and began to repeat it to myself until I felt peace: *When my heart is overwhelmed, lead me to that rock that is higher than I.*

God began to clear my mind and speak to my heart about what to do. I called my ex-brother-in-law who had recently divorced my ex-sister-in-law. He had phoned me within the last few weeks to let me know that he had been saved, so I called him. David not only came to my aid but he also agreed to pick up my waterbed and put it together for me the next day.

If you feel overwhelmed today, recite this scripture until you feel peace. God is our deliverer, our strong tower who we can run to for safety when the storms of life swirl and blacken our soul. He is our Prince of Peace during times of trouble. He knows the number of hairs on our heads, so how could he not know every single trial that we face? He is teaching us to run to him, trust in him, and let him be that strong tower for shelter during the storms.

As one of my Lifehouse women used to say, "Don't give up when you could just be thirty seconds away from a miracle."

Dear God,

I feel overwhelmed today because of so many circumstances. I have nowhere to run to, so I choose to run to you, my strong tower. You know what I need. You know how to get it to me. Let your Holy Spirit minister peace, comfort, and direction today. Open my spiritual eyes, ears, and heart to receive from you. I bind the enemy of my soul and his plans for me this day. I trust you, Lord, because I know that you are able. Nothing is too difficult for you. Amen.

LORD, HERE I AM

Lord, here I am with a heavy heart.
Please take these things that tear me apart.
The doubt, the fear, the unbelief;
these are the causes of my grief.
Infuse into me your Holy Spirit.
Tune my ears to your voice so I can hear it.
Open your arms wide to me.
As I come running, set me free.
Take all my garbage and my fears.
With your gentle touch, dry my tears.
Please turn up that Holy Spirit fire
to burn out all the muck and the mire.
Holy Spirit, cleanse my sin
as I freely invite you to enter in.
Turn my tears into seeds;
for you supply all my needs.
Dear God, I need you, oh so much.
I desire the tenderness of your touch

HAVE MERCY, GOD

"Let the wicked man forsake his way and the evil man his thoughts. Let him turn to the Lord, and he will have mercy on him, and to our God, for he will freely pardon."
—Isaiah 55:7 (NIV)

My ex-con friend, who I'll call *Joe*, was one of the most influential men in my Christian life; however, he was also the man with the most colored, sinful past I ever encountered. God brought him across my path to teach me many truths.

Joe had been convicted of over twenty armed robberies. He had escaped a maximum-security prison. When recaptured in Michigan, he was told he would never be released from prison because he was a habitual offender. God had other plans for him, though.

One day, a little old lady came by his cell and told him about the love and forgiveness of Jesus Christ. *Joe* accepted the Lord as his savior that day. He was determined to live his life for God, even if it was in prison. He studied the word for hours daily and began to preach to others in prison and lead them to the Lord.

Imagine his surprise when he got release papers from prison. Evidently, another prisoner had written to the parole board on his behalf, telling them how my friend had ministered to him and changed his life. Just like that, he was released from prison!

After being released, he joined Teen Challenge in Michigan. Since he was a recovering drug addict, he decided that this was where God wanted him. It was in Teen Challenge that he learned many tools for sobriety, freedom, and Godly living. It was also there that he met his wife.

Joe and his wife moved to our area, where her family resides. This is when I met them. *Joe* worked as a welder with my first husband. He and his best friend began to come out to our little mobile home and teach Bible studies to us and a few of our friends. We went to their homes for food and fellowship. I never left *Joe* without feeling that I had been touched by God.

After losing his job as a welder, *Joe* worked as a security officer at a K-Mart that had just opened. He told me this in case I was ever shopping and saw him shopping with another woman, his boss. They would shop together to catch shoplifters. Doesn't God have a sense of humor? You see, the last robbery that *Joe* and his friend had planned before returning to prison was to rob a K-Mart. Now *Joe* was serving as a security guard at another K-Mart.

The story grows more miraculous. *Joe* was interviewed by the US Postal Service for a job. They told him that they did not know why they were interviewing him because he was a convicted felon, and they had never hired a felon before. Not only did they hire him but they later promoted him as a counselor to those in the postal service who were in crises or dealing with addictions. He was head of the program in an area that spanned three states.

My friend was a lost man with an evil heart who turned to God for mercy.

God not only pardoned him and gave him freedom; he allowed his past to promote his future. Isn't that awesome? He will not only pardon you but will work everything to be for your good. Just trust him. He is a God of mercy.

Lord,

You know what I have done. Show me your mercy today. Forgive me of all my sins. Save my soul and help my life glorify you. Amen.

THE GREATEST GIFT OF ALL

He gently came to me in my agony and despair
When there was no one to turn to, or listen, or care.
As I wept and was overwhelmed with pain and grief,
The touch of his nail-scarred hand brought relief.
He gently wiped the tears from my brow.
With a gentle, healing voice said, "I am here, now."
He looked at me with soft but penetrating eyes
That said, "I know your past and sinful lies."
But not once did He scorn or even condemn,
*This one called **Jesus** offered to free me from sin.*
He said, "It's simple, but it wasn't cheap.
I gave my life so that for your sin, you'll not reap.
You don't have to accept the pain or go to hell.
I paid the price … I died for you. I did it well.
Come now, child, and run to me.
I want to love you, eternally!"

YOU MUST FORGIVE

"But if you do not forgive, neither will your Father, who is in heaven, forgive your transgressions."
—Mark 11:26 (NASB)

Looking back on my life, I see how closely God held me. He loved me enough to teach me very important lessons at a very young age. I remember one spring morning waking up and finding a red, raised, infected spot on my stomach. It hurt to touch it, so I showed it to my mom. She began to press and squeeze on it until a pine needle, about an inch long, popped out. I lived in the middle of a very small town, between the post office and barber shop, so the only opportunity for my exposure to pine needles was during Christmas. This pine needle had been in my stomach for over three months until it had become infected.

Years later, after going through a divorce, I began to study rejection and the importance of forgiveness. God showed me that when we are hurt or rejected by somebody, deep roots form and cause our soul to become sick or infected. Those roots have to be removed, or squeezed out, just like that pine needle from my stomach. We do not even realize that they are there until the infection makes itself known by manifesting in some kind of soul sickness, such as depression, anger, anxiety, fear, addictions, or rebellion. The key to deliverance from these is forgiveness.

God went on to show me that not having a whole sexual oneness with my ex-husband was because of being molested as a four-year-old. For me, sex was not the beautiful gift that God had intended for husband and wife. For me, it had been painful and dutiful. I had to ask God to forgive me and help me to forgive my molester in order to get healing from that infected pine needle that had formed in my soul. And He did just that!

> *Dear God,*
>
> *I ask that you show me any pine needles or infections in my soul. I give you the permission to bring them up so that I may confront them, deal with them, and be healed and whole as you have intended. I ask that you manifest forgiveness within my soul for those who have harmed me. I thank you for your faithfulness, perfect timing, and patience as I grow in your grace. Amen.*

I WANT TO BE A KAT!

"Whatever you have done to the least of my brethren, you do also unto me."
—Matt. 25:40 (KJV)

I have a wonderful friend who oozes with the love of Jesus. She doesn't only hear and know the word of God; she lives it. She is such an example of how Jesus would live here on earth that a family member calls her Saint Katherine. I call her Kat.

I remember how much she and her husband ministered to me during and after my divorce. Two such times will forever be engraved upon my heart and mind. She would be embarrassed by my giving her any credit, so I will give the credit to the spirit of God who dwells richly within her. I hope these stories will encourage and motivate you as they have done for me.

After my divorce, I finally got a minimum-wage job to support myself and my two little ones, so I had need of a babysitter. I didn't, however, have the money for one until I got paid. Kat said that she would be happy to watch Joie, four years old, and Jenna, who was around eighteen months old. She had two boys of her own whose ages fell just after each of my children, and she agreed to wait for her pay.

The first week, I drove the kids to her house. The second week, she insisted that she bring her boys to my house to watch the kids so that it was easier on me. Not only did she take excellent care of Joie and Jenna but she had supper prepared for us when I got home. When I got my first paycheck, she refused to let me pay her.

Kat listened to me and prayed for me. She is such a gentle, soft-spoken, caring soul. Kat looked for ways to minister to me, and I will never forget what she and Bob did for me one Christmas. I was feeling sorry for myself because I would be alone on Christmas, would have no special gifts from a husband, and would not have money to celebrate the way our little family had in the past.

At work, that Christmas Eve, I was having a real pity party. That's when I got a call from Kat asking me when I would be home. I told her that as soon as I got off work, I was going to stop and buy diapers and would then come home. She tried to persuade me to forget the diapers and just come home, but I stubbornly persisted in my own plan.

Shortly after I arrived home, there was a knock at the door. When I opened it, there stood Kat and her husband, Bob. With tears in her eyes, she said, "Diane, we have a few things here for you from the Lord. We don't take any credit for this. This is the Lord, and we prefer that you not tell anybody that we did this." (Sorry, Kat!)

There were at least six bags of groceries containing diapers, snacks, and foods the kids ate, along with holiday foods for us. She had searched my cabinets while she babysat the kids for me so that she knew what I used and the brands that I bought. This brought me to tears and gave me joy at the same time. My God had not forgotten me. I was not alone at Christmas. He was still my provider. He had used Bob and Kat as vessels of his love. They were Jesus with skin on. Bob and Kat motivated me to remember others who are going through trials. I remember all that they did to bless me. I tried to pay the love of God forward as they did to me. I pray that the following poem will also motivate you to do the same. God gave me this poem when I was at a spiritual retreat, and I dedicate this to all the Kats in my life. Kat, thank you for being Jesus with skin on!

JESUS WITH SKIN ON

Help me be "Jesus with skin on" today.
Equip me, Lord, for whatever comes my way.
Soften my heart so I can feel their pain.
For someone to lean on, I'll be their cane.
Open my eyes so I can see the need.
Prepare my path, Lord. You, take the lead.
Open my ears to hear your every word.
Help me spread joy like a happy songbird.
Help me be "Jesus with skin on" today.
To see others' burdens and take them away.
Let me be the hands that are eager to give.
I want to give the hopeless a reason to live.
Fill my mouth with words that bring relief.
Open my arms to comfort those in grief.
Teach me to die so that others may live.
When I am offended, help me forgive.
I truly want to be "Jesus with skin on today!"

THE NAME OF JESUS

"Give thanks to the Lord, Call upon His name."
—Psalms 105:1 (NASB)

One summer I decided to take my two young children on a mini vacation to spend some time with a high school friend and her children. This was a **huge** step for me because I had never ventured far from home. Since I lived in southern Indiana and was traveling to Kettering, Ohio, this was to be my first solo long trip.

I was nervous, to say the least, as we packed the car and prepared to leave. We prayed with Jeff, my husband, before leaving him home alone. We asked for God's protection during our journey and that he would keep his healing touch upon Jeff while we were away. After some hugs and kisses, we were on the road to our destination.

After finally getting into Ohio, I experienced lots of road construction on the interstate. This didn't help my anxiety at all. Not only was I driving in a strange place but now I was being blocked in the fast left lane. With a concrete barrier on my left side and fast-moving, congested traffic on my right side, I had no choice but to stay exactly where I was.

I thanked God that my children were sleeping in the back seat and couldn't cause any distractions. That's when it happened, the moment of utter helplessness. A semi decided to get into my lane of traffic and didn't see me in his blind spot. I had nowhere to go because there was a concrete wall on my left, a speeding semi on my right, and congested, high-speed traffic in front and back of me. This was it! This was the moment that my children and I would meet our maker.

All I had the time or ability to do was to call out Jesus! It was as if everything was put into slow motion instantly. As I put on my brakes and braced for impact while heading for the concrete wall, I was shocked to see what happened next. It was as if the semi shrank to three feet, was synchronized to my exact speed, and the few feet in front of me became ten feet. Somehow, the semi made it into my lane without causing a ten-car pileup and killing the three of us. The angels stationed around my Ford Taurus did an awesome job because the near disaster was completely averted.

My son, Joie, awoke in the back seat when I cried out, "Jesus!" He witnessed the whole thing. He said, "Mom, Jesus saved us!"

My savior, Lord, friend, protector, miracle worker, Jesus Christ had done exactly that. He saved us once again. He came through when there was no possible way of escape for us. Nothing is too difficult for him, absolutely nothing!

Friend, are you in the middle of a difficult situation where there seems to be no way out? Are you pressed in with nowhere to go? You don't even know how to pray. You may feel trapped like a caged animal. What should you do?

The most powerful weapon in your arsenal for defense is the name of Jesus. All you have to do is call it out. Sometimes all I can do is to repeat *Jesus* over and over until I feel his peace. He has *always* come through for me and has never forsaken me.

Pray with me. *Jesus, Jesus, Jesus!* Friend, he has just moved heaven and earth for you. He has just touched your very soul because you called on the most powerful name in the universe!

THE NAME OF JESUS

Jesus, the name above all others...
The name that heals my sisters and brothers.
Jesus, the Prince of Peace...
That name of power, I now release.
Jesus, the great truth revealer...
He's the mighty sin concealer.
Jesus is my very best friend.
He's the beginning and the end.
He's the King of Kings and Lord of Lords.
Serving Him has great rewards.
At the name of Jesus, demons flee,
As He brings His grace and victory.
Nothing remains as before.
Our savior, Jesus, has won the war!

ORDERED STEPS

"In his heart a man plans his course, but the Lord determines his steps."
—Proverbs 16:9 (NIV) (If you want to hear God laugh, tell him **your plans**.)

When I was in high school, I wanted to go to a vocational school and study food preparation/sanitation. I talked to my guidance counselor about it, and she greatly discouraged me. She told me that I was too petite to handle all the large pans and equipment and thought that I had other talents and gifts I needed to utilize. After asking my dad about going to the vocational school, he told me, "No." That was that. I didn't go.

After graduating high school, I married and entered the work force immediately. I was a great student and could have earned scholarships had I tried to go to college. This is a choice that I often regret. For many years, I had a recurring dream. In this dream, I was walking down a school hallway looking at the lockers. I was back in high school. I thought that I probably dreamed about this because of my regrets for not continuing my education.

After my son started kindergarten, I began working at our local school corporation. This was the same school that I had attended. My children were also there. I started as a teacher's assistant and then advanced to the manager of food services for the middle and high school cafeterias. I worked in this school corporation for over fifteen years.

One day, as I was taking my deposits to the bookkeeper in the high school office, I went a different route to get there. I looked up and noticed that I was walking down a hallway that was filled with lockers. I realized that these were the lockers in my dreams. I heard the Lord say to me that I was exactly where he wanted me to be and doing exactly what he wanted me to do. Wow! Such peace came over me with that realization.

I was able to be off when my children were off school. I was able to be there for them, at their own high school, involved with their teachers and peers. I was the sponsor for the student Bible club that met every Tuesday. I was the sponsor for Fellowship of Christian Athletes and the leader of the student prayer group that met before school each morning to pray. I was there to encourage the students who came to me for prayer about their problems. I was exactly where God wanted me to be at that time, doing exactly what God had called me to do in that season of my life.

God had nudged me in that direction while I was in high school. Even though my counselor and dad had blocked that path, God still got me where I needed to go. Isn't he an awesome God? Even if I make a few wrong choices or turns, God can still make it right because I have a willing and obedient heart.

One of the students, who had been active in the Christian groups that I sponsored, is a missionary to the Muslim nations. Another of my students is a youth pastor. Another young man joined the armed forces to protect our nation. Some are teachers, youth leaders, and worship leaders, serving God in many capacities. God used me to encourage these young people to become what he had called them to be.

Even though I was not college-educated, rich, or famous, I was doing exactly what God had called me to do in that season of my life. I was contributing to God's kingdom and the things that really matter. I was making a difference in those lives and the lives that they touched.

Don't let Satan get you down by looking at others' lives. Don't let him tell you lies about messing up, making mistakes, and being worthless. God is bigger than those lies, our wrong turns, and mistakes. Just surrender your paths to him today!

Lord,

I surrender my past, present, and future to you. Please direct my paths and erase all my regrets. Amen.

CHANGE THEM...OR CHANGE ME

"Change my heart, oh God."
—Psalms 51:10 (NASB)

When I was growing up, my mother disliked animals. She was the type who made us wash our hands if we touched a cat or dog, so having a house pet was definitely out of the question. I grew up with this mindset, so I agreed with her rule about no house pets.

When my daughter was about to turn sixteen years old, she asked if she could have a dog. My husband had agreed, so I was okay with an outdoor pet if she took care of it herself.

Imagine my surprise when I discovered that her dog was to be an indoor pet. I was livid. The dog was not yet trained, so it had several accidents on my new carpet. It chewed up shoes and did everything that is normal for puppies to do. I decided that since the two of them had teamed up against me that I should just move in with my mother who lived just across the road from us.

I did have a nudge from the Holy Spirit, so I did at least pray about it. I said, "God you are going to have to change Jeff's heart or my heart because I can't live like this anymore." Guess whose heart was changed?

Our pastor and his wife taught us how to potty train Weston using the crate or pet carrier. That improved things somewhat, but I was still not totally happy about the situation. When Weston did something wrong or chewed up something he wasn't supposed to, we always said, "Weston, go to your house." And he did. Then it got to the point that if he vomited on the floor or did something he thought was wrong, he put himself in his house.

Gradually I began to see how smart, loving, and faithful our little Weston was. For at least three months, he never even barked. We began to think that he was not capable of it, until the day he finally barked. It scared him and us. He became a part of the family. I was falling in love with him because he would sit beside me and look up at me with those beautiful sad eyes. When my husband was sick, he always laid right beside him on the couch. He sensed that Jeff needed him. When Jeff was hospitalized, I didn't have to come home to an empty house because Weston would be there waiting for me.

I realized that God had changed me in a big way. I now had an adorable dog who was three-fourths Boston terrier and one-fourth Chihuahua who lived in my house. He loved us. He loved chewies, long walks at the park, sleeping under blankets, playing tug-of-war with a toy, and playing fetch. I had gone from a dog hater to a dog-loving pet owner. Wow, God had done a big work in me, so much so that when our daughter married, the dog stayed with us. I was blessed with ten wonderful years with an awesome, loving dog. It broke our hearts when he suffered terribly from prostate cancer before his death.

We are so busy trying to change everybody else that we forget to ask God to change us. We are the only ones over whom we have control, so if we are willing to allow God to change us, he does! That's the question for today. Are you willing to allow God to change your heart? If not, you may miss out on a blessing.

Take a minute to ask God if there is something that he wants to change in you. Ask him to show you what it is. Do you always have to be right or have the last word? Are you critical? Do you have a tendency to gossip? Are you argumentative? Have you been holding a grudge? Has God identified pride, anger, resentment, or unbelief? If you are honest, like everyone else, we have a need for God to change us daily.

Pray this with me.

Change my heart, oh God. Renew that right spirit within me. Make me more like you. I give you permission to show me the sin within me and ask that you change it. Make my heart like your heart. Make my words like your words. Change my love into the way that you love. You are the potter, and I am the clay. Change me and make a beautiful masterpiece of my life. Amen.

THE PROTECTOR

"Though I walk in the midst of trouble, you preserve my life; you stretch out your hand against the anger of my foes, with your right hand you save me."
—Psalms 138:7 (NIV)

Losing my first parent to death was a trial I won't forget. My dad had been diagnosed with lung cancer in November of 1992 and died just two months later in January of 1993. It was after 2 a.m. on that cold January morning when my dad went to be with the Lord. My almost twelve-year-old son and nine-year-old daughter and I were taking my mother home from the hospital to spend the remainder of the night with her. That's when it happened. "Bang! Bang!" we heard. Was it a blown-out tire? What was it?

As we were driving down Broadway Street in Louisville, Kentucky, right in front of the White Castle restaurant, we were being shot at by a sniper. Could this really be happening to us, just moments after enduring the painful passing of my beloved father? What was I to do now? I missed my entrance ramp in the excitement of the gunfire. I was going to turn back in order to get there but my daughter cried, "No mommy, they will shoot us."

This put me into the west end of Louisville in the wee hours of the morning. I followed the detour signs that would have taken me to the 22nd Street entrance ramp, but the signs ceased to exist. This was not a neighborhood in which we needed to be lost at this time of night. I asked God to help me find my way because I was tired, nervous, mourning, afraid, and lost.

Just a few moments later, I saw a police car at a gas station. I pulled over to ask for directions to the interstate ramp. When he began to instruct me to go two blocks north, one block west, etc., I asked him if that was left or right. He looked at me as if I were a bimbo. I said, "Look, my father just died. We were just shot at back at White Castle. I just want to take my family home."

The officer looked at me with compassion and understanding and said, "Follow me," and he gave me a police escort to the entrance ramp.

Where was God in all of this? He was right there with me as my comforter, protector, and guide. God doesn't promise us we won't have any trials, but he does promise to go through all the trials with us.

Remember to count your blessings in the midst of the mess. I started to count my blessings later as God reminded me of them.

1. My dad only suffered two months from lung cancer before his death. His suffering was minimal compared to countless others.
2. Dad was a born-again believer rewarded with heaven.
3. God protected Mom, Joie, Jenna, and me from being shot that day.
4. God answered my prayers by sending a police escort to guide me to my entrance ramp.

Are you afraid today? Do you need a protector or comforter? God promises that He will be there for you. Just as he protected us, guided us, and comforted us, he will do the same for you. Just ask him.

Dear Lord,

I need your protection, guidance, comfort, and healing today. Thank you for your promises to me. I know that your Word does not lie and that you are able to do everything you have promised to me. Amen.

WHO DO YOU SERVE?

"Choose for yourselves today whom you will serve; but as
for me and my house, we will serve the Lord."
—Josh 24:15 (NASB)

I awoke one morning in tremendous pain. It was one of those days that made me think about doing nothing but lying in bed, tuning out the world and all the events of the day. It was one of those days that makes you want to throw in the towel and give up. Doesn't sound too spiritual, does it?

I had been diagnosed with rheumatoid arthritis years ago and have undergone all the modern medical treatments, including chemotherapy, Enbrel, Remicade, massage, warm water therapy, herbal solutions, and countless others. Just recently, I was diagnosed with fibromyalgia. Both of these disorders cause intense pain and exhaustion. If I let them, they can rule my life. This is an ongoing, daily struggle for me.

Some days are better than others, but this was not one of them. I had my seventeen-month-old grandson, who I needed to watch while my son mowed my grass. This was the last thing that I physically felt like doing, and I was to the point of tears at the thought of facing my day. While preparing blueberry pancakes and sausage for their breakfast, I truly had a pity party for myself.

Then I began to talk to the Lord about my pain, and this is what I heard in my spirit. *Choose ye this day whom ye will serve.* Are you going to serve the pain or me?

Will you let it control your day or let me guide your day? *Ouch!*

I then began to rethink what I had done and said that morning. I was whining and complaining because I had to serve my husband, son, and grandson. I was angry and short with them because I resented the fact that they were able to enjoy a run, or go to a meeting, or play with toys while I had to serve in my pain and exhaustion. I voiced my feelings, not in a very nice tone, I might add.

God had, with a very gentle nudge, reminded me that I was not serving Him but was serving my pain today, and the choice was mine to make. I then remembered how Jesus served the very disciples who were about to betray him or deny ever knowing him by washing their feet at the last supper. He didn't complain, knowing the suffering he was about to endure. He did it because he loves us so very deeply that he served us with his life and suffering.

I asked God to forgive me for my bad attitude and help me to be like Him by offering my suffering up to him as a sign of my gratitude and love for what he had done for me. By doing this, I made a choice to serve God, even in my own pain and suffering. I asked Him to help me, give me strength, and touch my physical pain.

He did all of those things for me. I made it through the day with God's strength and help after I asked for it. I had to mentally and physically make a choice, though; otherwise, I would have allowed the pain to rule over me. I would have become a slave to my pain, but I chose to be a servant of the living God.

Are there days you struggle with pain, resentment, unforgiveness, addictions, or other life-controlling problems? It is okay if you do, because God knows our pain and suffering like no other can. He knows what is on our mind and heart before we do. He knows our every weakness and remembers that we are a work in progress. He has the answer for every problem, but the choice is ours to make. Are we going to serve Him today or our problems?

Dear Lord,

Help me to serve you today. By faith and obedience, I choose to do that instead of what I feel like doing. Help me. Strengthen me. Guide me. Amen.

Things I Do to Overcome Pain

1. I remember those in worse shape than me. Then I pray for them and thank God that I can overcome because of what He has already done for me.

2. I think of somebody going through a trial and send them a card or give them a call.

3. I turn on praise music to change the atmosphere of my thoughts and home.

4. I pray and ask for God's help. He often leads me to scripture or gives me poetry.

5. I light an aromatherapy candle and take a warm, long bath in my whirlpool tub. Oh, I am so thankful for my tub!

6. When in unbearable pain, I call and ask others to pray with me and ask for God's touch.

7. When possible, I get a massage. This relaxes all my muscles and lessons the pain tremendously.

8. I cook something special for a family member or friend.

9. I always praise the Lord, whether I feel like it or not.

10. I put my feet up and meditate on the goodness of God.

DEAR LORD, I LOVE YOU!

Oh, dear Lord, I love you,
So much I can't explain,
And I choose to exalt you
As I lie here in my pain.
God, I need your presence,
Like the soil needs the rain.
I know my secret longings
For you are not in vain.

Like a fresh, empty sponge,
My soul soaks you in.
Your awesome holy presence
Floods my spirit once again.
Like the falls of the Ohio,
You wash away my sin.
I feel the nearness of you
Like a protective mother hen.

No matter what I face today,
You are the missing link.
As the problems may befall me,
In your presence, I will sink.
You are always the right answer,
Regardless, of what I think.
So I choose to love and trust you
Just as naturally as I blink.

NEED WATER!

"As the deer pants for the water brooks, so my soul pants for thee, oh God."
—Psalms 42:1 (NASB)

In 2000, I was told that I had a tumor on my pituitary gland and that I needed surgery. Since the pituitary is at the base of the brain, this can be a very risky procedure. The neurosurgeon who was to do my surgery told me about the risks involved and emphasized the gravity of my situation. He told me that the tumor would be removed through my nose, and if all went as expected, I should be in and out of the hospital in three days. I wasn't really worried about the surgery because I heard the Lord tell me, "You will live and not die."

As I told my sisters and other family members about the surgery, they voiced the concern that they would be gone on vacation. I told them not to worry and to enjoy their family vacation together. I did not realize that I was headed for a battle for my life.

After school was out for the summer, I headed into surgery one May morning. I had been bathed in prayer and was only slightly nervous. I checked in for a 6 a.m. surgery and did not awake until after 5:30 that evening. I was in intensive care, and everybody seemed to be very concerned. I didn't know why until the next morning, though.

I was putting out about a gallon of urine an hour. This was not normal by any means, so they sent me to a connecting hospital for an MRI to see what was going on.

I will never forget my nurse that day. His name was Chris, and he was kind, young, handsome, and very good at his job. He had to push me in my hospital bed, with all my machines connected, through the halls to the connecting hospital.

I began to have an insatiable thirst that I had never before experienced. I needed water as much as I needed every breath. Chris had to stop at every water fountain we passed because I needed to drink in order to satisfy my thirst. When they put me into the MRI machine, they told me that it would be quite lengthy and that they would pull me out halfway through. In the meantime, they would be able to hear me if I needed anything. I kept saying, "Need water." Finally, they pulled me out and put a straw through the mask that had been placed over my head to keep me still. I never needed a drink of water as badly as I did at that time. I knew what it meant for a deer to pant for water. It was life itself that I was seeking.

I was told that my brain had swollen as a result of the surgery and had damaged the part of the brain that puts out the hormone that signals the kidneys to work correctly. My kidneys would not shut off as a result of it, and I was truly dying of thirst. At 2 a.m. one morning while in intensive care, my veins collapsed. I was going into shock because of dehydration, and the nurses couldn't find a vein for my IV fluids. The person in the unit across from mine was pulling out his tubes and walking around naked. The nurses had their hands full with the both of us needing immediate attention. They had to call a person from radiology to put in an emergency port for my fluids.

I remember lying there asking God to not let me die alone. Then I remembered the still small voice that had told me, "*You will live and not die.*" God's peace came over me, and the port was successfully placed.

I spent five days in intensive care and five more days in the hospital. This was a far cry from the three days I had expected. I was told that my insatiable thirst and massive urine output were because I had developed diabetes insipidus. I was released from the hospital giving myself shots to regulate the disorder and then graduated to a nasal spray. This spray signaled my brain to regulate the kidneys in a normal way. I was to take it morning and night and skip one dosage weekly to avoid overdosing. I would need to do this the rest of my life. This was the cure for my thirst. It was vital for my survival, and I was told never to be without it, or I could die from dehydration.

I now knew true thirst, the life-threatening, I-can-die-without-water kind of thirst. I thought to myself that this must be how the deer felt when he panted for water. He had to have it to survive. That is exactly how my soul longs for, seeks, and desires the Lord. I have to have him to survive the trials of my faith and my life. Without him, it's not possible. I long for him to the core of my very being. The good news is that he is there to save me from death, hell, myself, and trials of my faith, if I only ask him. "*Those who hunger and thirst for righteousness shall be filled*" *(Matthew 5:6 (KJV))*.

Dear God,

My soul thirsts for you today. I need you, God. Help me in all that I do so that I can glorify you with my life. Infuse into me your spirit, your love, and your grace because without you, my soul will die. I choose life today, not death. I choose you today, Lord. Amen.

PRAY FOR KENNY

"If you believe, you will receive whatever you ask for in prayer."
—Matthew 21:22 (NIV)

My sister, Chris, always calls me when she has a need because she believes that I have a direct prayer line to the Father and that He always answers me. I just believe that God hears and answers prayers. It was her daughter, Sherri, who received a miraculous healing when I prayed as just a child. Chris knew that God could do miracles, so she called and asked that I pray for one.

Her husband, Kenny, had been given some very bad news. He was told that he had kidney cancer. This was especially bad for him because he only had one kidney remaining. His surgery was going to be very risky. They didn't know if the kidney could be saved. They didn't know if the cancer had spread to any other organs. She was afraid of losing her husband long before his time, so I told her that I would pray.

I arrived at the hospital while the surgery was in progress. The waiting area was filled with his children, their spouses, his grandchildren, sisters-in-law, and a few brothers. Kenny was in no short supply of those who loved and supported him. It was a very serious, somber group I had joined.

The surgeon came out to explain that they were able to save half of his remaining kidney. They had gotten all of the cancer, and it had good margins. It had not spread elsewhere. What remained to be seen was how his half of a kidney would function. Only a miracle would make it do what two kidneys were supposed to do. Dialysis was not yet ruled out, and his recovery time would be hard and long.

Kenny said something very wise to his wife before surgery, "We prepare for the worst and hope for the best." That was over eighteen years ago now. Kenny never had to go on dialysis. His half kidney, which was actually called one-fourth of a kidney, has miraculously functioned better than any doctor would have imagined. Kenny is still farming. He's still taking his children and grandchildren on vacations to Myrtle Beach every year. God heard and answered our prayers better than we could have expected.

I have no magical ability in my prayers. I only read and believe what the word of God says. God can do the same for you when you pray and have faith that He will do what the word of God says He will do.

Are you in the midst of circumstances that seem impossible? Are you afraid? Has the devil told you that God never listens when you pray? You are not alone. The Bible teaches us that Satan lies and he hopes that we believe him.

God listens when we pray and answers each and every prayer. Sometimes it may not be in the way we think He needs to answer. It may not be as soon as we'd like the answer; however, He always listens and answers. He will listen to your prayer today. Take a moment to voice that deep concern to God and trust Him to answer it. God cares as much for you and listens as intently to you as He listened to and answered our prayers for Kenny.

Many years after I wrote this about Kenny, the cancer came back and spread throughout his body. He underwent radiation and chemotherapy with one-fourth of a kidney. It still functioned until God called him home to rest. That first surgery that removed the cancerous kidney gave him extra years of enjoyment with his family. He took the entire family on vacation each year. They made precious memories. He got to see his children, grandchildren, and great-grandchildren. They all loved and idolized their Pap. We love you Pap and will see you again one day in heaven.

BREAD OF LIFE

"Then Jesus declared, 'I am the bread of life. He who comes to me will never go hungry, and he who believes in me will never be thirsty.'"

—John 6:35 (NIV)

Earlene had lost her job, and her husband had just retired from the armed forces. Needless to say, funds were really tight. One morning, during Earlene's prayer time, she asked God to meet her needs for gas money and bread. He answered quickly and rather uniquely.

As she was driving down the highway, she got behind a bread truck that was driving under the speed limit. Suddenly, the back door of the bread truck flew open. Imagine how surprised and elated Earlene was to see loaves of bread flying out the back door. The driver kept going, totally unaware that he was losing bread. Earlene pulled over and picked up the loaves of bread that had not burst open from the impact of hitting the highway.

Not too many minutes later, as she was pulling into the parking lot of a mini mall, she saw money floating through the air. The wind stopped and deposited it at her feet.

One of the names of God is Jehovah Jireh, meaning "our provider." The scripture says that we have not because we ask not. Earlene had asked God to meet her needs, and he did as she requested. Wow, don't we serve an awesome God?

What do you need? Is it monetary, spiritual, a heart's desire, a physical healing?

Do you want to be more like God? Is Jesus your best friend? Pray with me.

Dear God,

You know exactly what I need today. (Name it out loud to him.) I know that you are able to meet every need. I believe but help me with my unbelief. Teach me to trust you. Increase my mustard seed faith. Help me to know you as my provider, healer, and Prince of Peace. Amen.

THE INSTRUCTOR

"Whether you turn to the right or to the left, your ears will hear a voice behind you saying, 'This is the way; walk in it.'"

—Isaiah 30:21 (NIV)

F or a few years after my divorce, I prayed that God would restore my marriage and my family. I did this until one night I heard my little son ask Jesus to send him a new daddy. It broke my heart and caused me to pray. I surrendered my wishes to God and asked him to do what was best for my children. If their daddy wasn't going to come back to his faith, then I would accept another man as a daddy for my children. I knew that this was something that I desired and Joie and Jenna needed.

For a while, I dated other men. They never seemed to work out. Either their relationship with God wasn't right, they didn't want a ready-made family, or they didn't like me as much as I liked them. After some frustration, I decided that I would give up men for my New Year's resolution.

I had a New Year's Eve date planned with a nice, fun guy who was a body builder. He respected me and had never done anything but kiss me on the cheek. It was to be a clean, fun, safe last date. After all, I was giving up men after that night.

God had different plans, though. A Christian brother invited me to join him, his wife, and some others from our church at his home. He said he had a man who had recently been saved and would be perfect for me. He was thirty-two years old and had never been married. Marvin said his friend knew that I was divorced and had two children and still wanted to meet me.

I prayed about it and decided that God wanted me to cancel my date and go to Marvin's New Year's celebration. That's where I met Jeff. He was tall, dark, and handsome with a neatly trimmed, stylish mustache and big smile. He had a good sense of humor and we enjoyed playing cards together. We brought in the new year of 1987 together. While every other couple shared a kiss of celebration, we awkwardly smiled at one another and looked at the ceiling.

Jeff asked if he could call me for a date sometime. I didn't have anything to write my number on, so I handed him a bank deposit slip with all my info. Of course, this was before all the electronic bank frauds. He laughingly inquired, "Do you want me to make a deposit while I'm at it?" We parted with him saying that he would call me. Having heard this from others before and being disappointed on numerous occasions, I replied, "We'll see."

Jeff did call and asked me out on a date for the following weekend. After that, he took me out to lunch after church. We disclosed everything to one another on that date. He told me about his past drug and alcohol addictions and that he had been sober for the last three years. I told him about my divorce and my two children. We each expected the other would have been turned off by our honest disclosures but were pleasantly surprised when that did not happen.

One Wednesday evening, Jeff called to ask me if he could pick me up for church. I told him that I had the kids. He inquired, "Is that a problem?"

I responded, "It isn't for me if it isn't for you."

This is when he said the line that won my heart: "I would hate to think I would be so narrow-minded that I would let something like that stand in the way of a relationship. If it is meant to be, it will all work out."

I thought to myself, "Wow, a real man!"

Jeff met the kids that night. While I was readying them for bed after church, they disappeared. I found them in the living room with one sitting on each side of Jeff's lap as he was reading them a book. It melted my heart for the second time that night. About six months later, we married. Jeff told everybody that he barely made it under the wire. I had decided to give up men for my New Year's resolution, but God had other plans for me when I finally surrendered plans of my own.

What do you need to surrender today? Are you sure your plans are God's plans? Just take this time to listen to his voice so that He can tell you if there is something you need to surrender or change.

Lord,
I surrender all to you. Nothing will I hold back. If I have, show me. Amen.

BETTER PLANS

"However, it is written: 'no eye has seen, no ear has heard, no mind has conceived what God has prepared for those who love him.'"

—1 Corinthians 2:9 (NIV)

M y husband, Jeff, has an awesome testimony of how God saved him from death on numerous occasions, set him free from drug addiction and alcoholism, and then saved his soul. It all started because of the prayers of his grandmother and another little lady.

Jeff started drinking at the age of fifteen and using drugs at the age of eighteen. At that young age, drinking and using drugs became the only thing of importance to him. It dictated his life and almost took it on several occasions. Each of the near-death experiences were because of drugs and alcohol. He had been arrested on several occasions for alcohol-related charges.

Jeff was involved in several car accidents while under the influence. He fell off a fifty-foot cliff at Clifty Falls State Park while hiking under the influence. Even though he broke his back, fractured his hip, and compressed two vertebrae (which shortened his six-foot-one-inch height to an even six feet), he escaped death. He could have been killed during his alcohol-induced fall at Clifty Falls State Park but miraculously was not.

On another occasion, he was thrown out of a moving vehicle that was traveling at over eighty miles an hour. He just so happened to land in the yard of a registered nurse who kept him alive until the ambulance arrived. Three of his five vital signs were not present at the time because he had ruptured his spleen, and over 80 percent of the blood in his body was in his abdominal cavity. He made it through surgery and out of the coma it left him in. Another miracle!

During his last drunken stupor, he blacked out and hit a car with a man and woman inside. He was at home asleep when the police arrived to arrest him for a hit-and-run accident. This was trouble that his dad couldn't get him out of. Mothers Against Drunk Drivers had just formed, so stronger penalties were being sought for drunk driving. As he laid in jail that night, he prayed with sincerity. He told God that if he would help him get out of this situation that he would get sober. God did, and Jeff did!

Jeff joined Alcoholics Anonymous. It was there in the twelve-step program that he came to know about a loving and caring God. God cared enough about him to want him to be sober. After being sober around three years, Jeff gave his heart to the Lord during a service at my church. Not long after, we met and married.

Jeff was a talented and gifted musician who used to play his guitar in bars. He decided to play his guitar at church for praise and worship. He also began to play in a Christian rock band called Midnight Cry. One weekend, Midnight Cry played at a youth event in a park in New Albany. There he met the man and woman he had run into in his last drunken stupor. Their son was the youth pastor of the church who had organized the youth event.

The couple came up to Jeff and introduced themselves. The precious lady said that when the accident happened and she was lying in the emergency room that God had told her to pray for that young man. She had been doing so ever since. She said that she was so thankful he had gotten saved and was now working for the Lord. God heard her sincere prayers.

God had performed many miracles for Jeff before he was even a Christian. God knew that Jeff was going to love and serve him in the future, so he protected, prepared, and loved him through the darkness.

Friend, you have no idea what glorious thing God has prepared for your future!

What he did for Jeff, he can do for you. He can make a masterpiece out of your life. All you have to do is to ask him. If you have loved ones who have not yet surrendered their lives to God, don't give up. Don't stop praying for them. Be like Jeff's Grandma Priscilla, who never quit praying for him and never gave up on him. Somewhere down the road, you will also see answered prayers.

Dear God,

Please continue to draw _____ with your Holy Spirit so that they, too, will acknowledge you as Lord and Savior. Amen.

SCARS INTO STARS

"Since you are precious and honored in my sight, and because I love you."

—Isaiah 43:4 (NIV)

Jeff, my husband, is a gifted musician. Even though, he has had very few music lessons, God has given him the ability to hear music and play it. He plays piano, bass, acoustic, and lead guitars. His favorite instrument of all time is his Gibson Les Paul electric guitar. This guitar was given to him by the Lord, more than once.

His first and favorite Gibson Les Paul was given to him by the church in which he was saved and married when his Gibson SG Deluxe was stolen during a robbery. The replacement was a white Gibson Les Paul with gold pickups. Jeff says that guitars in heaven will look just like this. Imagine his utter shock and bone-chilling disappointment when it was destroyed one worship service. He tripped over the cord, causing the guitar to lunge forward from the stand onto the floor. The neck was broken completely in two.

When God calls a person, he also equips them. God didn't want Jeff to quit playing worship music, so he made sure Jeff had a guitar. The first thing that happened was that the church members decided to pay for the expensive repairs.

A few days later, when an old friend called and heard Jeff's guitar horror story, he had a solution of his own. At the same time as Jeff's Gibson Les Paul had been given to him as an insurance settlement from the church robbery, this Christian brother had bought an identical guitar of his own. He had long since replaced it with another and was keeping the original in a closet as he sought the Lord about what to do with this prized guitar. Mark told Jeff that now he knew he was supposed to give it to him.

Jeff was blessed to see how much the Lord wanted him to continue playing his guitar for worship, so he did. He played the precious gift that Mark had given him until his original guitar was repaired. When it came back from the music store, he was quite disappointed with the repair. An ugly scar was very visible where the guitar had been broken; however, it still had the sweeter sound of the two guitars.

Jeff was playing the scarred guitar during a youth worship service one evening, and it produced heavenly sounds. These sounds resonated throughout the church as almost angelic. The Lord spoke to my heart about scars at that time. He showed me my own scars. I had a large scar on my wrist from a third-degree burn. I had one where the tip of my middle finger had almost been severed. I had scars on my eyebrow, abdomen, thumb, shoulder, and ankle from surgeries. I had scars on both elbows from a bicycle accident. Even though my body was a mess of scars, God was not finished with me. Quite the opposite was true because he was turning my scars into stars.

You may ask, "What do you mean by this, Diane?"

The word of God tells us in Matthew 5:16 (KJV), "*Let your light shine before men so that they may see your good works and glorify your father which is in heaven.*" When we let our scars become testimonies of the overcoming power of God, they become stars that shine for him. Joseph said to the same brothers that left him in a hole for dead, "*as for you, you meant evil against me, but God meant it for good, to bring it about that many people should be kept alive, as they are here today*" (Genesis 50:20 (ESV).

Just because Jeff's scarred guitar didn't look as good, it didn't mean that he was finished making beautiful music with it. As a matter of fact, it still sounded better than the shiny, unharmed, more valuable guitar that Mark had given him. God asked me then, "Do you want to look better or be used by me?" Ouch!

Now I ask you the same question. I also ask: Do you have scars in your life that have made you feel as if God is finished with you? If so, they are lies from the enemy of our souls. Today, offer these scars up to God as overcoming testimonies of his healing power. Let him turn your scars into stars that shine for him and may encourage another brother or sister along the way.

Remember that you are precious and honored in the Lord's sight, even with all your scars.

Dear God,

Forgive me for doubting and being confused by the scars of my past. I forgive those who have caused these scars, and I offer them up to you today. Take these scars to bring me healing and to use as a testimony of that healing in my life. Help me not be afraid to share these testimonies with others so that you can turn my scars into stars that shine brightly for you. Let my scars give hope to other hurting people and remind me daily that you are not finished with me yet. Amen.

MMM GOOD!

"Oh, taste and see that the Lord is good."
—Psalms 34:8 (NIV)

I live in the country, in what used to be a corn field. We have a two-acre yard, two-thirds of which is in the backyard. I used to walk my dog, Weston, around the border of my backyard in the summertime. Weston and I both enjoyed this variation in our walks.

One day I noticed some blackberries beginning to grow in two or three patches along the edge of the property, so I started taking a small bucket to pick some berries as Weston and I walked. My son loves blackberry cobbler or crisp, so I would freeze them little by little until I had enough to do some baking.

That hot cobbler with a little ice cream on top was worth the effort I had put into picking the berries.

Early one morning, as I was walking and picking some berries, the Lord began to speak to my heart. The scripture, "Taste and see that the Lord is good," came to mind. Then he began to show me that nobody had planted those blackberries. They were a free gift for me to enjoy. I did have to pick them, though, or I would not be able to enjoy the gift. He said that's like salvation. "It is free. I have already paid the price, but not everybody chooses to enjoy it or receive it. Salvation is just like those blackberries. Unless you taste and see that they are good, you have no idea of the gift I have given to you."

Wow, I thought about how wonderful, sweet, and generous our Lord is. He made the blackberries, and all I have to do is pick them and enjoy them.

Salvation encompasses more than just saving our souls from hell. It also encompasses provision, comfort, healing, mercy, and a relationship with our Lord. We can choose to accept all of the benefits or stop short with having our names written in the Lamb's book of Life.

As I was walking each day, I began to see more blackberries. There was an abundance of large, juicy ones just beyond my reach. In order to get to them, I had to go through briars, take the risk of getting chiggers, mosquito bites, and pierced skin. Was it worth the risk? It depended on how badly I wanted all the fruit. The Lord began to show me that many Christians stop short of the best, juiciest fruit, or gifts, because they do not want to take the risk or apply the effort.

I asked the Lord, "Do I do that?"

He replied, "Sometimes. I have so many good things in store for you, my child, but you need to press on. Don't be stopped by the thorns, mosquitoes, or chiggers. Those represent the enemies of your soul, and I have given you power over all power of the enemy. Nothing shall by any means harm you, so stop being intimidated so that you do not miss the best I have for you. That is not my plan."

Have you tasted of the Lord's goodness? If not, today is the day of salvation. It is simple. It is free. It is wonderful! You only have to pray this simple prayer with me and mean it. Whether this is your first prayer for salvation, a recommitment to the Lord, or help to reach the unreachable fruits or gifts, the Lord will meet you right where you are.

Dear Lord,

Thank you for dying for my sin and for the free gift of salvation. I admit that I am a sinner in need of your full salvation plan. Please forgive my sins and give me the strength and courage to reach for the best that you have freely given to me. I want my life to glorify you, Lord. I want to fulfill the purpose for which you have created me. I humbly ask for your mercy, grace, and help. Amen.

THE GREAT SHEPHERD

"What man among you, if he has a hundred sheep and has lost one of them, does not leave the ninety-nine in the open pasture, and go after the one which is lost, until he finds it?"

—Luke 15:4 (NASB)

M y husband, Jeff, has a love for nice ink pens. One such ink pen is a wooden pen with a cross and scripture in the middle of it. When he loses or misplaces one of his pens, he won't stop searching for it until it is found. He moves couch cushions, enlists my help, retraces his steps, checks shirt pockets, whatever it takes to find the missing pen. He will not stop until it is found. This sometimes drives me crazy because, to him, finding that missing pen is more important than anything I happen to be doing at the time. One day, as I began to get agitated by another search and rescue for a missing pen, I heard that still small voice say, "That's just like me."

I asked the Lord what He meant, and He said that He is the great shepherd. When one of His sheep strays or gets lost, He does whatever it takes to get them back. I never understood why the missing ink pen was so important to Jeff, since he had countless others that could be used in its place, until God spoke this to my heart. Even though God has countless others who choose to serve Him, He still seeks and saves the lost. He loves and cares for us so much that another could not take our place. He loves us enough to look for us, search diligently, and draw us with his Holy Spirit to the point that He never gives up His pursuit of us. When I realized this, I realized how much God must love us.

He loves and cherishes us more than Jeff cherishes his ink pens. I know the trouble that Jeff goes to for his lost ink pens. He doesn't stop until they are found. Isn't it awesome that our God pursues us that faithfully because he loves us so much? Wow!

This means that He will not stop seeking you and searching for the missing parts of your heart. This means that He cares as much for your lost son or husband as you do.

This means that you are very valuable and dear to Him. He will continue to draw you closer and closer so that He can whisper sweet secrets to you and will allow you to hear that still, small voice. He will continue to give you the "milk" of His word that will cause you to grow up into the child of God He has called you to be. Finally, He will teach you how to draw others unto "Him."

The Lord would say to you today, "Little one, do you not know how much I love you? Do you not know how valuable you are to me and the plans that I have for you? Do you not know how much I need you to accomplish my purpose for your life and the others that I love? Come to me today. Let me love you, guide and direct you, and do an awesome work in your life…because I want to…because I have great plans for you."

Pray with me today.

Jesus,

I surrender. I surrender all to you today. Be my great shepherd. Continue to search for_____, my lost loved ones. Draw them with your Holy Spirit. Shine your light on their hearts and on mine. Amen.

A TIME TO WEEP

"I would have despaired unless I had believed that I would see the goodness of the Lord in the land of the living."
—Psalms 27:15 (NASB)

Our pastor taught from the book of Ecclesiastes, which teaches that there is a time for everything." We all enjoy laughter, but nobody enjoys the tears; however, those tears are as essential as the air that we breathe. The tears teach us compassion, faith, endurance, humility, how to have peace in the midst of the mess, that God is very near to the brokenhearted, and how to trust Him no matter what comes our way.

Pastor James also said that others may be in a different season of their lives than we are at the time, so we are not to force our season on them or to take their season on as our own.

Yes, we are to weep with those who weep, but we are not to replace our season of laughter with their season of tears, or vice versa. You see, God has a specific reason and lesson for each season of our life.

I remember one particular season of tears in my life. It seemed to go on and on. It was as if I had become flooded with a monsoon of tears. Everything in my life was hard. My husband was near death. My children had moved in with their dad and new stepmother. We were having financial problems paying medical bills and other unexpected financial emergencies. I felt like giving up. I felt as if God had forgotten me. The devil had me convinced that I must have committed some great sin that caused God to be punishing me. Sound familiar?

When I visited another church, the pastor shared the above scripture, "*I would have despaired unless I had believed to see the goodness of the Lord in the land of the living.*"

This scripture taught me many things. First of all, if the follower of Jesus could feel despair and hopelessness, it was possible that I, too, could feel despair. God had not forgotten me. The devil was telling me that my life would always be this way, but this was another one of his lies.

I could have hope in the future, and I wouldn't always be crying. The key for me was to believe in the goodness of the Lord and to praise him in the midst of my messes. Then God could turn my mourning into dancing. He could turn my sadness into joy. He could give me hope instead of hopelessness. He could teach me some very crucial lessons in the midst of the mess. He could hold my hand and dry my tears. I could know God in a new way and give others hope, even during my time of weeping. God was not far away but very near to me because I was brokenhearted. God knew and understood my pain and would never leave or forsake me.

Are you in a season of tears right now? Have you felt like giving up lately and that things will never change for you? If so, pray this with me.

Lord Jesus,

You know where I am right now. You even know the number of tears that I have shed. You know that I need you, now more than ever. I am sorry for doubting you and for listening to the lies of the enemy. Take my tears and teach me. Show me how to get closer to you. Bring healing to my life, and once again, show me your goodness. Amen.

THE FAITH WALK

"We live by faith and not by sight."
—2 Corinthians 5:7 (NIV)

I endured an excruciating, never-ending trial that lasted over two years. It grated on my spirit like an aching tooth that would not quit its throbbing. This trial involved one of my most prized and cherished possessions: my daughter, Jenna.

Keep in mind that I had two miscarriages and a stillborn daughter before I was blessed with my children, Joie and Jenna. I had endured five pregnancies to have my two children and had watched my brother bury his two babies. I realized that children were precious, miraculous gifts from God and were not to be taken for granted.

When Jenna was five months old, her daddy left the three of us. I was remarried to Jeff when she was a little over two-and-a-half years old. He called her his "pookie" and never treated her like anything less than his own flesh and blood.

Jenna was a great student, an obedient daughter, popular, cute as a button, a child to be cherished. Then she turned thirteen. Suddenly she became argumentative when we said "no" to anything. On one such occasion, I responded, "When you live in our house, you live by our rules." Her solution to that was to call her "other" dad and tell him to come and get her. She moved across the river to Louisville, Kentucky halfway through her seventh-grade year of school. She moved in with her biological father, who was going through another divorce and shortly thereafter had already moved in with another woman.

When it became obvious that she was not coming home and that it was not a fleeting response, Jeff and I were heartbroken. I felt angry, rejected, and shocked, and I questioned God. I asked God, "You already have three of my children in heaven, why do I have to lose her too? What have I done so wrong? Why, God, why must I lose her to the very man who left us? Hasn't he taken enough from me?"

This is where my journey of faith began. I attended church more. I prayed more. I did everything that I could to get closer to God because only *He* could get me through this time in my life. I knew that my daughter was not in a Christian environment in the most impressionable, formative time of her life. I was afraid of what could happen to her. I was afraid that I could lose her forever. I was afraid that my life would never be the same again.

One Sunday while attending church, I turned to the text for the sermon. The text on the adjacent page jumped out at me. Jeremiah 31:16–17 (NCV) read:

"But this is what the Lord says: 'Stop crying; don't let your eyes fill with tears. You will be rewarded for your work!' says the Lord. 'The people will return from their enemy's land. So there is hope in the future,' says the Lord. 'Your children will return to their own land.'"

I had been shedding a lot of tears, so you can bet this verse spoke to me, loud and clear. I especially noted the part about my daughter returning to her own land. I took this as God's spoken promise to me in regard to my daughter. I decided to mark it, stand on it, and believe it. This is what I was hoping for and not yet seeing. This is where my faith met the road. (The story will be continued in the next devotional.)

Dear God,

Help me to remember to live by faith instead of what I feel or see. Help me remember that things are not as they appear. Amen.

HELP ME BELIEVE!

"I do believe; help my unbelief."
—Matthew 9:24 (NASB)

O ftentimes when we take a stand, the devil works harder to make it not come to pass. This was no exception for me. For months I continued to get my daughter every other weekend and to listen to how happy she was. She loved her school, had plenty of friends, had made the cheerleader squad, and talked constantly about her dad's new girlfriend. She told me how much she liked her, how fun she was, how pretty she was, and how all her friends thought that she was really cool. Then she told me how her dad had gotten married again and how neat the wedding pictures were.

It was very hard for me because I felt such rejection and dishonor. It was especially hard when I was attending a women's retreat on Thanksgiving weekend. I received a call from my husband that the kids' father was there moving Joie out so that he could live with him also. Now I had lost both children.

I went back to the scripture that said, "***Your children will return to their own land.***" God already knew what was coming when He gave me that word. Even though the battle had become more intense, the promised outcome would still be the same if I continued to pray, wait, and believe.

Their dad had initiated court proceedings to get legal custody of the children. Around this time, Joie decided that living at his dad's was not where God wanted him to be. When he returned home, I realized that I had won half the battle. The battle for Jenna became more heated because she was awarded to her dad for legal custody.

I kept saying that Jenna would be home one day. She told me that she was happy there and that she was never coming home. My son told me that I should get it through my head that Jenna was never coming home. I told him that God had promised me she would, so I was standing on His word instead of what I was hearing and feeling.

I then went to my bedroom and started crying. I asked God about the scriptures he had given me and if I should hold on to them. I heard the still, small voice say, "Things are not as they appear." Even though I was unsure of what this meant, it gave me comfort.

Within two weeks, I received a call from her dad saying that he was going to bring Jenna to church to meet us and give her back. He said his marriage was more important and that we could have our daughter back. Hallelujah!

Oftentimes the battle becomes more heated and intense right before the victory. The enemy of our soul does this to get us to fall into doubt, unbelief, and discouragement so we lose sight of the faith-given victory that could only be a day or two away. This is what Satan tried to do with me, but I continued to stand on the word of God that was given to me in the beginning of the trial. Even though it took two years to be completed, God returned Jenna in a way that closed the door for her ever moving back in with her dad again. God did just as He had promised me.

Are you encountering doubt, fear, or unbelief because of your circumstances? Rest in God and on His promises and pray with me.

Dear God,

I know what you have promised me, and I do believe. Help me with my unbelief, doubt, and fear. Forgive me, God. Help me to focus on your answer instead of my problems. I declare that I do trust in you and in your promises. Amen.

TAKE CARE OF ME?

"Therefore, there is therefore now no condemnation to those who are in Christ Jesus."
—Romans 8:1 (KJV)

After experiencing some rapid, irregular heartbeats and chest pain, it was time to go to the doctor for some tests. I discovered that it was stress and a poor physical condition. It was a wake-up call for me. Since my husband was so ill, I knew that I needed to take care of myself, or I wouldn't be around to take care of him.

I called a Christian counselor who was recommended to me by many others. She helped me see the importance of taking care of myself. She told me it was okay to have fun, get a massage, join the YMCA for exercise, and explore my God-given gifts and talents. She said it was okay for me to go out to lunch with friends. These things would help relieve stress.

During one of our sessions, I was talking about the death of my mother. My mom was very ill with lung cancer during the 2003 holidays. She was admitted to a nursing home for the last week of her life because we were unable to lift her and care for her as needed since the cancer had also spread to her brain.

During that same week, I had a hysterectomy scheduled so that I could get it in before the end of the year. This helped me avoid another $8,000 deductible that would become effective on January 1 of the next year. I knew in my heart that my mom would die while I was in the hospital. I talked to her about my surgery, and she said to go on and take care of myself. She knew how badly I needed the surgery, so I went on as scheduled.

I was admitted to the hospital a few days before Christmas, after having Christmas with Mom and the kids. I took her gifts to the nursing home (some of my baked ham and cookies) and promised Mom that I would see her again. In my heart, I knew deep down that it would be the last time I would see Mom on this earth.

I had the surgery, which happened to be more extensive than expected. I was cut from hip bone to hip bone for the complete hysterectomy and bladder repair. On Christmas morning, my brother called me and said that my mom was having a rough time. She was holding on so that she could see me and make sure that I was okay. I was still her baby, and she was still a concerned mother. He asked me if I would talk to her, so I did.

I told mom that I loved her and that the surgery went well. I told her that I might be going home soon, but it was okay for her to go home now. She had fought a good fight. She had been a great mom. It was okay for her to join my father in heaven, and I would see her again one day. A few hours later, my brother called to say that Mom was in heaven now.

It was Christmas morning. I was told that my mother had died. My doctor came in to say that I was being released with a catheter for my bladder and told me I would not be up to attending a funeral. My husband and children attended Christmas dinner at my sister's, as was tradition, but I stayed home to rest and heal. I was lonely, grieving, and in pain physically and mentally.

As I tearfully shared this story with Tess, my counselor, she told me that I needed to take care of myself. Let God take care of my time to weep. This was more healing for me. During our prayer time, she asked that God would give me a vision or a poem about Mom's entry into heaven so that it would bring me peace. The following poem is what God gave me as a result of her prayers. I hope it will bless you as much as it has blessed others during their time of mourning.

Let us pray together.

Dear God,

You know my faults, my mistakes, and my weaknesses, and I know that you died for all of them. Forgive me once again. (Name your sins or mistakes as God brings them to mind). Remind me that they have been covered by your blood when Satan tries to bring them up again. Help me to overcome these bad feelings about myself so that I can take care of me. This will give me more time and strength to take care of my family. Bring me complete healing so that I can be the person that you have created me to be. Amen.

MOM'S CHRISTMAS DAY

The red carpet was laid at Heaven's gate.
There were friends and family there to wait
to welcome dear Mom on that Christmas Day.
At the front, Jesus himself led the way.
He said, "Welcome home, little one.
Your work on earth is finally done.
Enter in at heaven's door,
receive your crown and blessings galore."
She saw countless mansions on streets of gold.
And banquet tables with delicacies untold.
Only moments before, she said goodbye to me.
Now she was pain- and cancer-free.
Greeted by those who had gone before,
She realized her dreams and even more.
No more pills to take or bills to pay,
Mom was present with God all the day.
The flower gardens made her dance and sing
as Heaven's joy bells began to ring.
The flowers were giants when compared to earth.
With jeweled borders, who could tell their worth?

There were tulips, pansies, and species unknown
that were vibrant as the Lord's light was shown.
The fragrance was sweet, unique, and rare.
The beauty of God's garden was beyond compare.
Mom danced with glee but had praises to say
as she joyed in the Lord on that Christmas day.

MY SAVIOR SPEAKS

"If you remain in me and my words remain in you, ask whatever you wish, and it will be done for you."
—John 15:7 (NIV)

One of my shifts at Lifehouse included taking some of the pregnant young residents to a baseball game to see the Louisville Bats play. We were blessed with tickets by somebody who wanted to bless Lifehouse. We were excited because it was something out of the ordinary.

We also had money to get a snack and a drink. Once we purchased those in a long line, we found our seats. Soon after, the game started. The large bird mascot encouraged us to clap and cheer when our team did well. After a couple of innings, something happened that totally shocked me. One of our players hit a ninety-mile-an-hour ball, which came off the tip of the bat and hit me in the elbow. I ached and then started feeling numb. I felt a chip in the bone on my elbow.

I went to the first aid station to show them what happened. The nurse agreed that I had a chipped bone in my elbow. She said that they could put me in the ambulance and take me to the hospital. When I asked if the ballpark would pay for it, she said no. She said that if I looked on my ticket stub, in the small print it states that they are not responsible for accidents or injuries.

I had just gotten new health insurance. I was not sure if the coverage had yet started. I decided to wait until the next morning, after I got off work, to have it checked out by my local hospital. We drove to the drugstore, and I purchased a sling, a few ice packs, and some over-the-counter pain medications. Instead of feeling sorry for myself, I realized that if the baseball hadn't hit my elbow, it would have hit the pregnant young woman right beside me in the head or the stomach. She was ready to deliver in a few weeks. She could have lost the baby girl or ended up with brain damage. My chipped elbow was the least of the three choices, so I actually started to praise God.

When we arrived back at the Christian maternity center, we all readied ourselves for bed. I removed my clothes to put on my pajamas with much difficulty and pain. I was not even sure if I would be able to sleep, but to my surprise, I fell fast asleep. While sleeping, I had this dream. A man was sitting across from me at a table. He asked if I believed in healing as he slid the Bible across the table to me. I told him I did because if the Bible says it, I believe it. The dream was over as fast as it had begun.

The next morning when I awoke, I didn't move for a bit because I was concerned about my pain level. To my surprise, I had none. I went to the ladies' room and removed my sling. I moved my arm around and there was still no pain. I felt my elbow and found that the chip was no longer there. I had the young ladies feel my elbow, and they were amazed that there was no longer a chip to be felt. It made believers out of those who didn't believe in healing before this incident.

I had asked the Lord to heal my elbow so that I wouldn't have to spend all day Saturday at the hospital and probably pay for everything out of pocket. I think that God honored the fact that I believed what the Bible said about healing. I truly found out that God healed me because I abide in Him and His words abide in me, so I asked, and He gave me the healing. God is so good. He is a healer just as his word says He is.

Dear Lord,

I believe in you, your word, and your healing. You know my needs before I even ask. Help me to abide in you and let your word abide in me. When I ask for healing, a closer relationship with you, peace, or an increase in faith, I know that you can do it for me. Thank you, Lord. I love you.

IN THE MIDST OF THE MESS

"In all your ways acknowledge him, and he will make your paths straight."
—Proverbs 3:6 (NIV)

The lessons learned by my chipped, then healed, elbow continued a few more days. God continued to use it to teach and astound me. Here is the rest of the story.

On the following Sunday morning, Dr. Finley Baird came to our church to minister. During the praise and worship service, the Holy Spirit began to drop a poem in my mind. I wrote it down and knew that I would share it later in the service. Imagine my elation when Dr. Baird ministered about how we are to respond to trials in our life. He even went so far as to mention Shadrach, Meshach, and Abednego and how

Jesus was with them in the fire. When you read the poem, you will be amazed at how awesome God is. Dr. Baird even said that he had his sermon planned for weeks until God woke him up that morning and switched directions on him.

There is still more. For twenty-one years, I wanted Jeff to put music to many of my poems. God has enabled us to coauthor three songs now, but Jeff had not worked on putting music to the rest of them for many years. A man from a music store, who was present to help with the new monitors after church, sat behind me. He commented on the beauty of the poem. He looked straight at Jeff and said, "You need to put some music to that, brother."

We serve an awesome God! He is able and he is good, especially in the midst of the mess.

Dear Lord,

Help me to praise you even when everything goes wrong. You are still God in the midst of my mess. You still have a plan for me. Amen.

IN THE MIDST OF THE MESS

It's easy to praise when all is right,
when the sun is shining, and our future is bright.
But when trials abound comes the true test.
Can you praise the Lord in the midst of the mess?
Just like the fourth man walking in the fire,
Jesus is with us in the muck and the mire.
Just like the rope that saves from sinking sand,
Jesus is waiting with his outstretched hand.
Just like the music that soothes my soul,
God's spirit comforts and makes me whole.
When we begin to praise, it weakens Satan's hold,
and strengthens our faith to run for the gold.
When you're down and out, let his praises ring,
'Cause demons flee when we start to sing.
In all things give thanks, says the Lord.
When suffering's great, so is our reward
Our praises heal, like salt in the wound.
Then, with His spirit, we are tuned.
When your problems rise and you start to cry,
then praise the Lord, and He'll draw nigh.

It's easy to praise when all is right
when the sun is shining, and our future's bright
but when trials abound, pass the test.
Praise our God in the midst of the mess!

THE MIRACLE WORKER

"Always give yourselves fully to the work of the Lord, because you know that your work in the Lord is never wasted."

—1 Corinthians 15:58 (NIV)

When I became a house mom at Lifehouse, I had no idea what I was getting myself into. I knew that God had called and placed me there, but I did not know that it was both a blessing and a trial. God has used Lifehouse and the women I encountered there to teach me many things.

Most of the women came to us because they had nowhere else to go, as was the case with (let's call her Angie) one of my most challenging women to date. Angie came to us pregnant and single, and she brought her toddler with her. She came with the intention of having this baby and giving her up for adoption because she knew that she was neither equipped nor ready to raise two on her own.

Angie was beautiful, very intelligent, and a natural leader; therefore, she often set the tone of the house. Whatever Angie did or thought was always known, and the others followed suit most of the time. I seldom met a person with whom I could not get along, but for some reason, Angie and I clashed most of the time. No matter what I said, she took it offensively, and I thought that she had a bad attitude.

One week when bad weather had canceled school, all the young women at Lifehouse were home. They were working on puzzles, laughing, and having fun while I watched the toddler and went about doing chores and cooking. I had just received news that my husband could have cancer and that a good friend of mine had committed suicide. My mind and mood were not in the best place. I was fearful, mourning, sad, and tired.

After asking the ladies to help and reminding them to do their chores, they told me I was bossy, rude, and a few other things that I don't even remember. Needless to say, my current mood did not allow me to contemplate and act in a Christ-like manner. I said the first thing that came to my mind, and it offended Angie because it came across like I was criticizing her parenting skills. This was a tender subject for her, so things exploded from there. From that moment on, she and I rubbed each other like sandpaper.

I prayed about her and for her a lot. I prayed about my attitude toward her. I prayed for her toddler and for her unborn baby. God even gave me a poem for her. I asked God to show me ways to love her. I probably prayed for this young woman more than any other, yet I got along with her the poorest of all.

After going back to work full-time as a traveling sales representative, I worked less and less at Lifehouse, only two days a month. On one Friday afternoon after Angie had graduated from the program, she came to the house very upset. Only a few of the new girls and I were there. She needed to talk to somebody, and of all people, it had to be me. I knew that's what she was thinking when she arrived; however, she was in such turmoil that I was all she had.

I took her downstairs for some privacy and asked what was on her mind. She explained that this was the first birthday of the little girl she had given up for adoption and that her boyfriend had only upset her more instead of comforting her. They had argued, and that's why she ended up at Lifehouse.

Immediately, I asked if I could pray with her. I joined hands with her and asked for God's wisdom and comfort. I prayed that he would hold her as she mourned the loss of this little girl. Even though she knew she had done the best thing in the situation, she still hurt. I asked God to touch Angie and give her a clear mind about her boyfriend and to see things through His eyes instead of through her pain. Afterward, I hugged her and held her as she cried.

Soon after, she married the boyfriend and sent me wedding pictures. Later, she spoke at the Lifehouse Unity for Life fundraiser. I was privileged to hear her testimony of how Lifehouse and the people associated with it had changed her life. Through her time at Lifehouse, she had been born again, gotten baptized, received Godly counseling, gotten a full scholarship, learned to be an even better parent, placed her child for adoption to a good home, had married, and was getting ready to graduate from college. God had completely turned her life around. I had been a very small part of that, and it made me so proud of her. God had heard and answered my prayers. He had also healed the relationship between me and Angie.

This affirmed the scripture that our work in the Lord is never wasted. Americans live in such a microwave, drive-through society that we often forget that it takes time to see God's harvest. We get inpatient and doubtful. We stop praying and give up.

Have you ever done that? Are you there now? Do you have a lost son or daughter who doesn't seem to get any better? Do you have somebody who rubs you the wrong way? If so, pray with me.

Dear Lord,

You know that I have been praying for _____.
Things don't seem to be getting any better, and the enemy of my soul continually tells me that you don't hear me when I pray. Forgive me for doubting or giving up. From today forward, I will believe that my works for you are never wasted. I know that you are on the case and that my prayers are not in vain. Be the miracle worker that you are, Lord, and do the miracle for which I am praying. Help my faith grow stronger. Amen.

LOVE FROM A LIFEHOUSE
HOUSE MOM

I try so hard to show you that I care.
Am I wasting my time? Do I really dare?
When I am talking, do you even hear me?
We're both God's children, don't you see?
I am older and supposed to be the wiser of the two,
But there are moments, that even I don't have a clue.
Try to remember that we were purchased by the King.
God created us both, so let his praises ring.
On that cross, He died for me and you.
God loves us both. Yes, it's really true.
He says to love one another, but please tell me how
that I can reach out and show you God's love, somehow.
Just know that I'm here because of Jesus, our friend.
I'll be praying for you from now until the end.
I pray that you'll be happy and truly blessed,
Have a good life, and in his peace will always rest.
I pray that one day you will be loved by a Godly man
Who protects you, listens, and will fully understand.
May you be surrounded by God's undying love.

Then one day, you will thank our God above
For the short time that your life was touched by me,
The plump, silly woman who only wants you to be free.
Sweetie, please know that I really do love you,
In spite of what you say or do.

THE GREAT PHYSICIAN

"With men this is impossible, but with God all things are possible."
— Matthew 19:26 (NKJV)

E arlier in this book, I shared how surgery to remove a pituitary adenoma damaged my brain and caused a condition called diabetes insipidus. This surgery nearly took my life and caused me to spend five days in intensive care and another five days in the hospital.

I was putting out over a gallon of fluid an hour because the part of the brain that creates the hormone that controls my kidneys was damaged when my brain swelled after my surgery. I have lived since that May in 2000 on a nasal spray called DDAVP. One squirt every morning and evening would cause my kidneys to function properly. Once every week, I missed one dose to prevent an overdose. When I missed a dose, I always knew because I would start thirsting, drinking, and urinating.

My endocrinologist told me that I would have to be on this the rest of my life and that I was never to be without the medication and water. He said that I could dehydrate, go into shock, and die.

When this first happened to me, I asked God to heal me. The doctor told me originally that these things sometimes correct themselves; however, after six months had gone by, he said it wouldn't happen. If it were going to happen at all, it would have done so before then. My sister, Chris, said that she had always believed that God would heal me. It just had not happened, so I continued to purchase my nasal spray at over $300 for a month's dosage.

In November 2016, more than twelve years after my surgery, I had almost forgotten about those prayers and my desire to be healed. I had just accepted it and learned to live with diabetes insipidus.

Many, many years ago, something happened during one of our church services. One of the precious, more mature ladies in our church came over to me during worship time. Sue brought her prayer partner, Jan, to talk to me. She asked me if I had diabetes. I told her that I didn't have diabetes, but I had a disorder called diabetes insipidus. She said that the Lord told her He had healed me from it. I now only had symptoms of the disease.

Later in that same week, I was driving down the road in my sales territory when I remembered what Sue had shared with me. I felt the Lord prick my heart. I told God that if the Word was for me, I would happily accept the healing. I just didn't know what to do about my nasal spray. If I stopped using it all of a sudden, it could mean a life-and-death situation for me. I asked him to help me know what to do and not to doubt a miracle if that is what He was doing.

Not long after, I started forgetting to take my nasal spray. Mind you that any time I missed a dose, my body would always tell me. I started the excessive thirst, drinking, and urinating when I missed the nasal spray. I realized that I had missed three doses without my body signaling my need. I started noting each dose that I missed with still no body signals to remind me. I have now been without medication for over five years. God has truly done a miracle and healed my diabetes insipidus. He answered prayers that I uttered over sixteen years ago and had given up hope of ever getting answered. Even my endocrinologist confirmed that I had received a miracle.

Satan will tell you that miracles don't happen today or that they do not happen to you. Don't believe or accept those lies. God is more than able to do things that man cannot do for us. He is not only able, but He is ready and willing.

What hope have you let die? What prayer seems too impossible to answer? Tell it to Jesus today. Believe that it is a possibility with him.

Dear Jesus,

I am sorry that I have forgotten that you are a miracle worker. Help me to remember that you are the great physician who can still heal today. God, heal me. Heal my broken heart. Heal my body, soul, and spirit. Amen.

BE A FRIEND

"A man that hath friends must shew himself friendly; and there is a friend who sticketh closer than a brother."
—Proverbs 18:24 (KJV)

L et me tell you about Gavin. He had a deep faith in God. He was a handsome, smiling young man of almost sixteen years of age. He was not a follower but a leader. He never met a stranger and was a real talker. Gavin had great influence on others. He was active in his youth group at St John's Lutheran Church.

Gavin was a hard worker. He did everything from putting up hay to driving tractors and working in Paw's store. He helped his dad get ready for the breakfast rush created by Lanesville High School students where he attended school until his death.

From a young age, he showed animals in 4-H and made a significant amount of money selling them. He saved all of his money to buy a BMW when he got his driver's license.

One night, he prepared for bed. He told his dad and Sharon goodnight and that he loved them. He told his sister, Skye, goodnight and that he loved her also and off to bed he went.

It was after midnight when his dad had a policeman knock on his door. No parent wants to hear what followed. Christopher was told that Gavin had been in an accident and didn't make it. His family didn't believe it because they thought he was downstairs sleeping. To their surprise, he was not. Gavin had a back door downstairs on his level. He had snuck out to go to a party and had met his ride at the end of the driveway.

His ride home was with two girls who were in the front seat and Gavin and another boy were in the back seat. The two young ladies had been partying hard, but Gavin had no drugs or alcohol in his system. The car was going too fast to make a turn so it went off the road and hit a tree. Gavin was killed instantly when his head went through the window and hit the tree.

About two in the morning, I received a call from my sister, Irene, whom he called Mam. That is what all of her grandchildren called her. She was in shock and was going to her daughter's house. I told Irene that I would meet her at Jill's. I arrived to find his sister, Skyler, and his cousin, Isaac, very upset. Isaac was only two months older than Gavin, so they were very close. Christopher, his dad, arrived about that time, along with his wife, Sharon.

My heart broke for my loved ones. I loved that young man. He would go to lunch with Mam and me. He offered to buy her lunch on numerous occasions because he was such a generous guy. He asked questions and talked about many things. Gavin was quite the conversationalist. He once asked his grandma, "Mam, couldn't you just give her a second chance?" That is such wisdom coming from a teenager.

There were so many visiting the funeral home that the funeral director said it was the most visitors who had ever been in attendance there. It was because Gavin was a good friend to so many. Through tennis and 4-H, he had friends at every school in the area. One of the other schools had to have counselors come in and help them cope with his sudden death. He made friends at Salem High School from watching his friend, Cassie, as she played volleyball and softball.

The young lady driving the car was at fault and Gavin's friends were angry at her, so much so that she moved to another school. My sister said maybe it was Gavin who was killed because he was ready to meet his Lord. She was not angry at the girl or unforgiving. She thought that maybe the other three teens were not spiritually ready yet. Gavin did not have to suffer a permanent brain injury or paralysis. It was Gavin's time to go, and he was ready to meet his Savior. These thoughts consoled her greatly.

He is at peace and is probably asking Jesus a million questions. We will see him again one day and all of his new, heavenly friends. This does not take the hurt away, though. Many, to this day, still mourn his death. They are angry about it also.

Gavin did more in his short lifetime than most ever get to do. He went hunting with his dad and Busy Bee workers out in Colorado. He went to Germany and learned all about Martin Luther. He saved money and bought what he wanted, including a car.

Most importantly, Gavin made friends from playing tennis, 4-H, youth group, work, and pretty much whoever he came in contact with. Gavin had friends because he was always friendly. He was the first to talk and others felt comfortable with him.

At the end of what would have been his sophomore year, a scholarship was given in his honor. The valedictorian of the senior class announced who won the scholarship. First, she talked about her experience with Gavin. She had just started going to Lanesville High School at the time. She was lost and couldn't find her classroom. Gavin saw her looking around. He asked if there was any way that he could help her and then showed her to her classroom. Gavin introduced himself and told her if she needed anything else, just to let him know. This young lady said that he made her feel welcome at a strange school.

Gavin was a friendly young man who never met a stranger. He would have done anything to help a person if it was within his power. Gavin loved people and was not ashamed to show it. He was the best type of friend because he didn't change who he was so that he could fit in. Gavin was just a friendly person who loved to wear bow ties. To be a friend, you must show yourself as friendly like Gavin did.

We love and miss you, Gavin. In the meantime, we know that you are still making friends in heaven.

Dear God,

I thank and praise you for Gavin's life. Take away the anger I feel while mourning the loss of those I love. Bring healing to my heart. Help me forgive and not play the blame game so that I can become friendly like Gavin. Let your light shine through me. Show me what true friendship is and help me to be that kind of friend. I want to be like you, Jesus, that friend who sticks closer than a brother. Amen.

TAME THE TONGUE?

"But no one can tame the tongue; it is a restless evil and full of deadly poison."
—James 3:8 (NASB)

Have you ever been around somebody with a really vulgar mouth? I have. It almost makes me feel as if I have to wash out my ears. That would not help the situation at all, especially since a man speaks out of his heart. If his heart is filled with evil, that is what comes out of his mouth.

No man can tame the tongue, but Jesus can. It is just like any other habit we struggle with. If an alcoholic or drug addict joins a program for their addiction, the first step is to admit that they are powerless over it (alcohol, drugs, a foul mouth, food addictions, etc.). We cannot tame our tongues, but God can. He will get to the root cause of your bad mouth. After all, that sharp tongue can injure others. He definitely does not want another child of His to be hurt by anybody else.

Maybe you are angry about something that hurt you or you have not forgiven an offense from a divorce or a friend. This can make you start throwing around slang. The more you speak it, the more it becomes a habit. Your bad mouth may cause your child to pick up those words because they think if Daddy can say it, it is okay for them to speak like that.

Talk to Jesus about it and about what is in your heart. He can tame the tongue and overcome evil with good. You must become aware of what you say so that you can correct your speech. Do you want to hurt others? Do you want to cause others to speak like you? Then pray with me.

Jesus,

Give me a heart check and reveal to me what is in my heart so that I can deal with it. You are my healer and deliverer. Heal my heart and deliver me from the negative, hurtful, and slang words. I want to be like you. Replace those bad thoughts and words with good ones. Amen.

WHAT A MESS!

"Give all your worries and cares to God, for he cares about you."
—I Peter 5:7 (NLT)

A situation or state of affairs that is confused or full of difficulties is one of the definitions of a mess. Since this part of the book was written several years after other parts of the book, I am able to talk about the pandemic of the coronavirus. If there was ever a mess, this was the largest mess I have ever known.

Who would have thought that Americans would be walking down streets wearing masks over our noses and mouths? Never in a million years would I have believed this. We in the United States of America have never gone without anything. Suddenly we could not find toilet paper, antibacterial wipes, masks, food, other paper products, and antibacterial hand gels. Restaurants and businesses were forced to close for a while. We could no longer gather with family for Thanksgiving or Christmas, have somebody with us in the hospital, see a loved one in a nursing home, or go out to eat with some friends.

This pandemic stole many things from so many people. Graduates of high school or college were not granted the right to celebrate that greatly anticipated event. Cruises, weddings, and vacations had to be canceled. Expectations were reduced for the lives that we suddenly had to live. We could not attend funerals of friends. Lives were lost. Jobs were lost so people went without food, electricity, recreation, and in some cases, a place to live. We were no longer allowed to leave the country or go to church until we learned more about the coronavirus. Our world seemed to stand still for a while. I kept feeling that it was a nightmare and I would wake up to a normal world someday.

We lost my husband's mom during the pandemic. This robbed us of the last four months of her life. We were not allowed into the assisted living facility where she was getting the help that we were unable to give her during this part of her dementia. We saw her through a window a few times until she stopped knowing us. We finally got to see her on the last two days of her life. I only wish that we could have had more time with Mom to show her how much she was loved.

I had several friends and family members who had the coronavirus. One friend was on a ventilator for a long period. We prayed and prayed for him, and God brought him through.

We really grieved when a close friend died of complications due to the virus. We are now past the one-year mark since the pandemic reached us here in the United States.

My sister, Irene, has worn masks for several years due to her severe asthma and weakened immune system; however, she contracted the coronavirus. She self-quarantined. When we met for lunch, we drove through to pick up the food and ate it in the car. She was the last person who needed to get it. If it had gone to her lungs and settled there, she would have died. So many of us were praying that she never had to go on a ventilator. Even though she spent eleven days in the hospital, God protected her life. God wasn't finished with her yet because she is such a kind person and still has more to do here on earth.

Now we have vaccines that may not be effective when the virus once again mutates. At least at this point we no longer have to have friends or family members go get groceries for us. I can actually go to a store and buy things instead of getting everything online not knowing if it will fit. My eleven-year-old grandson, Ryder, can come over and spend the night again. We missed him terribly when the pandemic stole that time with him. We now selectively can hug those we love again. If the coronavirus made you fearful or anxious, please pray with me.

Dear Jesus,

I give my fear and anxiety to you because I know that you care for me. Since the great God of the universe cares for me, I know that I will be alright. Place a hedge of protection around me and my loved ones. Let the scientists find a vaccine that will wipe out the coronavirus just like smallpox and polio were defeated. Lord, help my faith to overcome these obstacles. Amen.

A NEW ANKLE

"Fear of man will prove to be a snare, but whoever trusts in the Lord is kept safe."
—Proverbs 29:25 (NIV)

I had an ankle replacement during the pandemic. This was a very serious procedure, and I was simply dropped off at the hospital for my surgery. I was in a strange place, during uncertain times, facing the most difficult surgery of my life. I sure wished that I had somebody there with me. This truly was a mess for me to overcome only through the grace and help of God. The surgeon called my daughter and reported how things went with the ankle replacement. She then had to relay the message to my husband. I had to diligently watch for infection after one podiatrist canceled my surgery because he said that I could lose my foot.

This made me very apprehensive, and I could not live in pain like this. It kept me from enjoying my life and doing normal things. I could not take walks with my husband and dog like I wanted to do. I couldn't climb up and down the ladder to my pool. I lost hope of ever getting a new ankle.

The podiatrist who refused to do the surgery gave me another name of a person I could contact, but he said that this doctor might refuse to do the surgery also. Without hesitation, the orthopedic surgeon said that he could operate. He was a teacher at the University of Louisville hospital. He had done over 250 of the ankle replacements. Before the surgery was to happen, I had to undergo many tests. They tested my bone density, my heart, and my lungs. Special scans were done to determine the type of replacement that would be best. Measurements were important so that the ankle constructed for me would be a perfect fit.

I was told the surgery would not be done if I had a sore or raw place on my body. Because of the location of the ankle and the fact that it was the most difficult joint replacement with the longest recovery, I was apprehensive. It takes almost a year for it to totally heal.

I was going to a hospital I had not attended before this. I had a new doctor who I didn't know. I had never met his staff before this. I had nobody who could stay with me because of the pandemic measures at all healthcare facilities. My daughter dropped me off and gave the staff her phone number so that she could report to my husband when the surgery was over, and they called her.

Why was I afraid of men? Why was I afraid of the surgery? Why was I afraid of the coronavirus? Why was I afraid of losing my foot? It was ridiculous because I trust in the Lord. He is bigger than all of my fears. He is bigger than infection. He is bigger than my unbelief. If you have been where I am before in your life or feel this way right now, pray with me.

Dear Lord,

Forgive me for being fearful. Forgive me for not trusting you like I should. Help me to overcome my fears with more faith. Help me to focus on faith instead of worry. Show me the lies that I have believed so that I can replace them with truths. Thank you, Lord, for being patient with me. Amen.

THE NECESSITY OF NEEDINESS

"That I may know him, and the power of his resurrection, and the fellowship of his sufferings, being made conformable unto his death."

—Philippians 3:10 (KJV)

While I was in the hospital after my ankle replacement, I truly took part in His sufferings. When the numbness wore off of my surgery ankle, I experienced pain like I had never known. Keep in mind that I had two children naturally with no medications. I had a total hysterectomy and was cut from hip bone to hip bone while at the same time, my mom was dying. The nurse told me not to be a martyr and use my morphine pump. I only used it three times. I had a torn rotator cuff that was repaired. I had an arthritic thumb rebuilt. I had an emergency appendectomy with a burst appendix, which was very painful.

I was no stranger to pain. I had never felt this intense pain where it continually felt as if my foot had been cut off. That night, I text messaged, called my husband and pastor, and posted on Facebook for prayers to overcome this. I cried. I tossed. I put on the light for my nurse to come. I used my morphine pump, I was given a pain pill, and finally got a pain shot which reduced the pain.

When I was released from the hospital, I was told that I could not put weight on my ankle for two months due to the severity of the surgery. This caused great neediness for which my husband was responsible. I used a knee scooter that helped but imagine backing it into the restroom when you are in a hurry to go. Jeff had to prepare my meals, help me tie my shoes, and do all the household chores for two months.

Unless we allow God to help us in our neediness, we will never truly know Him. The more needs we have, the more opportunities we have to come to know Him. One can learn more about God in one night of pain than in a year of abundance.

God is who I cried out to in that night of pain. I came to know him as my friend, my healer, my helper, and the one who makes me strong when I am weak. I came to know him as dependable and faithful enough to hear my cries. I learned that He is with me through it all. I also learned to praise Him in the mess instead of complaining. That stops the devil right there in his schemes and plans to do harm to me. If you are in need right now or know somebody who is, pray this with me.

Dear God,

I really need you right now (in pain, anxiety, financial struggles, loneliness, or fear). I need to be close to you. I need to learn to trust you. I need to know you love me. I need a close relationship with you. I need for you to be my friend. Draw me close to you and never let me go. Amen.

MY MESS

I have made a mess of me.
Lord, now I give this mess to thee.
Take my heart and clean it up.
Take my life and fill my cup.
Turn the darkness into light.
Take the wrong and make it right.
Turn the bitter into sweet.
As every need, you can meet.

LOST PHONE

"For the son of man came to seek and save that which was lost."

—Luke 19:10 (NASB)

Recently I went to one of my favorite discount stores. When I was leaving, I wanted to call my husband and see if he needed anything. I noticed I did not have my phone. I emptied my purse, looked under the car seat, on the pavement outside my car, and went back into the store to see if it had been turned in. It had not. I even had the store call my number when I got back to my car. No such luck there either.

I decided to enlist my husband's help when I got home. He could not find it either. Jeff realized that I have the application to find my phone. After utilizing that application, it showed us the phone was back at the store. The next morning, we went back to the store to find my phone. He followed the phone dot around the store and outside where my car had been parked the day before. The store manager even helped him in the search. Still, we were not able to find it.

I am not an electronic whiz like my husband but decided to try my luck with it. I asked, "What does it mean if the dot and square are on top of one another?" He replied that I was standing right on top of the phone. I looked down, then under the shelf, still no luck. I tried calling the phone and heard a faint ring. After calling it a few more times, I found it inside a purse that I had examined the day before while I was shopping. Jeff had called me while I was shopping. I thought I had put the phone in my purse but had accidentally dropped it inside the purse in the store. Whew, what a relief!

We can't hide from God. He knows exactly where we are in the natural and the spiritual realm. Just like the good shepherd, He seeks us so that He can save the lost. He can also direct us back on the right track. He knows everything about us and where we are at the present time. God is even better than the application to find your phone. He knows our hearts better than we do.

Are you lost right now? Do you need to be saved from yourself, sin, or from hopelessness? Do you know without a doubt that your eternity will be in heaven? Have you gotten on the wrong path and need to find your way back to it? If so, pray with me.

Dear Jesus,

Thank you for seeking me out and drawing me in so that you can save my soul. I need for you to save me from my selfishness and my sin. I give you my heart today. I accept you as the son of God. I know that you died on the cross so that your body and blood would cleanse my sin. Thank you for never giving up on me. Draw me into a close relationship with you. I love you, dear Lord. Amen.

I AM WEARY AND NEED REST

"Rest, and be still."
—Jeremiah 47:6b (KJV)

Are you going through a tough time right now? Do you feel as if you have been hit with the sudden and devastating impact of a tornado? Have you hit a wall that will not be moved, or have a hurt that can't be healed? Are you discouraged, down, or wringing your hands? You have done all that you can do but nothing has changed.

Corrie ten Boom said, "When the train goes through a tunnel and the world gets dark, do you jump out? Of course not, you sit still and trust the engineer to get you through."

The Bible teaches that "*In the world you will have tribulation; be of good cheer, I have overcome the world*" (John 16:33 (NKJV)).

When I go through the trials of my faith, I always hear the voice of the enemy of my soul say these lies to me. "If you were living right, these things wouldn't happen to you." Sound familiar?

My train has taken me through dark tunnels of divorce, chronic illness and pain, the loss of three children, watching both of my parents die from lung cancer, financial difficulties, and having an ill husband that God could call home at any moment. My train has stopped in that dark tunnel on many occasions. I have learned to trust and rest in God because He has always come through for me. He works all things for my best. His timing is perfect. It might not be how I wanted or when I wanted, but it is better because it is in His time and will for me.

When you are in that dark tunnel, please know that God is already there waiting for you. He always has a plan and answer on the way. He knows how much you can tolerate and just what you need. He is just waiting on you to wait on Him. Just go to the heavenly Father and crawl up into his lap. Trust him to fix the broken things. That is how you rest. Rest in your daddy's lap.

Read his Word. My favorite book of the Bible during times of trial is Psalms. It is written by David who does his crying out to God when he is pressed on every side. He is also a poet just as I am a poet. Try reading Psalms and Proverbs in a month. Read three chapters of Psalms and one chapter of Proverbs each day. That will get you through both books of the Bible in one month and minister to you personally. It hushes the wrong voices and thoughts and increases faith in Him.

Your prayer for today is simple.

God,

Teach me to rest in you and to be still as I trust in
you. Amen.

WEARY WARRIOR

Weary warrior, take up your shield and fight
Cause Jesus, your savior, will strengthen your might.
Weary Warrior, don't give up or give in.
The one who loves you is stronger than all men.
For you are a soldier of the King.
He will guide you into battle and mark you with his ring
He'll give you marching orders and go on before.
God will fight the enemy and win the raging war.
Weary warrior, take up your shield and be still.
For your commander is mighty and His power is real,
Weary Warrior, hold your head up high.
Have faith, for your victory is nigh.

HAIR IN A BISCUIT

*"We remember before our God and Father, your work
produced by faith, your labor prompted by love, and your
endurance inspired by hope in our Lord, Jesus Christ."*
—1 Thessalonians 1:3 (NIV)

Oftentimes when I go to church or see a fellow Christian,
I am asked, "How are you?" I am careful with my reply
because *"Life and death are in the power of the tongue"* (Proverbs
18:21 (BSB)). Also, many believe that you confess the positive
answers about what God says. That is not wrong but for one
currently in the midst of the storm, that is not easy to do. For
those like me who continue to battle one health problem after
another or chronic pain, do we lie about how we feel? No, we
should never lie or feel beat up if we are in a trial.

When asked how I am doing, I almost always say, "I am hanging in there like a hair in a biscuit."

To me, it means I have been better, and I have been worse. This is a saying from down south that my sweet mother taught me. She used to bake homemade biscuits and gravy, fried pork chops, scrambled eggs, and hot apples for breakfast on Sundays or as breakfast for supper on some evenings. On rare occasions, one might find a hair baked in the biscuit. When this happens to your biscuit, you understand it is very, very hard to get it out of your biscuit if it was baked in the dough; therefore, you can now understand what I mean by that statement. I am hanging on to hope that it is in God's hands and **cannot be removed from His grip**. We can, however, let go of his hand and try to figure it out on our own. That is a particularly bad choice.

To me, hope is the prerequisite for faith. It is like the yeast needed for the dough to rise for making rolls or bread. One must first hope that things can change so our faith is born out of the need for a change. I see it as the fuel for faith. As God has answered in the past, those past answers make our hope and faith grow. This is easier to do if we shut out the bad thoughts and lies. Remember that the faith produced for this trial causes endurance for future battles. It also helps when others watch how we go through trials and persevere until we overcome the situation. Watching us overcome gives them hope and builds their faith.

Dear Lord,

Help me to hang in there during trials and to never let go of your hand. Increase my hope and faith in you so that

I can overcome whatever comes my way. Help my responses encourage others. Amen.

MY CONVERSATION WITH GOD

"What do you know?" God said to me
as I sat down with a glass of tea.
God, I know you love me and really care
Wherever I go, you're always there.
Yes, that's true, my little one.
Now think on things I've already done.
You saved my soul and you've been my friend.
You loved me, healed me, and provided without end.
Now tell me who I am to you?
Do you see me in the skies of blue?
God, you are the music to which I sing
and you, Lord, are my everything.
Now child, listen to the words I say.
I will turn your darkness into day.
I'll hold your hand when you are feeling blue.
I will never leave or forsake you.
I'll dry the tears from your eyes
and turn the storms into peaceful skies.

WHAT ARE YOU LOOKING FOR?

"You will seek me and find me when you search for me with all your heart."
—Jeremiah 29:13 (NIV)

I have a friend who went through divorce shortly before I did. He was very helpful ministering to me and gave me some really good advice. I will call him Mitch for the sake of this devotional. Mitch liked to share stories that were much like the parables of Jesus. Mitch had a very deep faith.

On one of the walks we took, Mitch told me about a strawberry patch that had ripe berries to be picked and weeds that needed to be pulled. The owner of this particular strawberry patch had very little time to do so. He decided to do both at the same time in order to save time.

The berry patch owner pulled some weeds for a while and realized that he forgot to pick the berries. Then he started picking berries but forgot to pull the weeds. Once again, he pulled the weeds and forgot to pick the berries. Mitch said the moral to this story is what you look for is what you find.

What are you looking for? Do you look for what is wrong about people, places, and things? If so, that makes you a very negative person. Do you look for what is right with others? If so, you are a very positive person. Do you look for miracles and testimonies or are you critical of everything?

If you seek God with all of your heart, you should be unselfish, positive and looking for good in others. By being this way, you will find the good in others, situations, and answered prayers. Do a heart check. Are you a complainer or one who praises? It will affect your life in a positive or negative way. Are you seeking God with all your heart or are you a lukewarm Christian?

Dear Jesus,

Help me to seek you with all my heart. Help me to look for the positive (fruit) instead of what is always wrong (weeds). Help my outlook bring forth good changes that come from you and let me always notice the things you have done for me. Lord, help me pick the berries so that I can stay in your will and bless others. Help me do what you would do. When there are weeds that need to be pulled so that the fruit can flourish, show me and help me. Amen.

STAND GUARD

*"And the peace of God, which surpasses all comprehension,
will guard your hearts and your minds in Christ Jesus."*
—Philippians 4:7 (NASB)

My friend, Mitch, shared another of his stories/parables with me. Both of us like to believe the best in people, which sometimes results in being hurt over and over.

He shared how everyone has an outer garden, a garden with a few vegetables in it, and then an inner garden that has beautiful flowers and luscious fruits. If you just barely know somebody, you may let that person in your outer garden.

If you know somebody and would like to know them better, you may invite them into your vegetable garden and send them home with some cucumbers. When we want to know somebody well enough to share secrets, or to see how much you have in common, we invite them into our beautiful inner garden. They can pick the flowers and the fruits. The problem occurs when that person hurts you over and over again because they can pick flowers and luscious fruits out of your garden. It becomes ugly, trampled, and empty. When that happens, we finally get smart enough to realize that friend is a user and needs to be thrown out of the garden before they pick it dry.

My heart can only take so much hurt and disappointment. If I continue to let people into my inner garden and allow them to hurt me over and over, it hurts more each time. My heart can become bruised and scarred. It opened my eyes to guarding my heart. I was a single mother of two toddlers. I was lonely and dating others who hurt me time and time again. I needed to put a fence around my inner garden and be very careful who I let in.

The Lord especially wants me to guard my heart because it belongs to Him. He does not want it to be trampled, unforgiving, or hardened. That is why He tells us to guard our hearts. He wants us to have peace. That is the key to all situations.

We need to trust him enough to have that peace that surpasses all understanding. He knows us. He loves us and moves mountains for us.

Lord Jesus,

Teach me how to guard my heart. Let me be discerning enough to be able to judge people by the fruits they bare. Give me hope and faith. Give me peace as I do this. Amen.

GOD IS OUR PROVIDER

"And my God will provide every need of yours according to his riches in glory in Christ Jesus."
—Philippians 4:19 (NASB)

I do not know one person who has never had a need. I know that I have had many. I was not born into money like some. No matter what our status in life happens to be, we will come to a crossroads when we need something that we are not able to provide for ourselves.

This is a chance for God to reveal to us that *He* is our provider.

It is not our jobs, our bank accounts, trust funds, or the lottery. The Bible teaches it is God. At times, God may choose to use some of those things to bless us and others, but we have to have monetary or specific needs in order to meet our provider, who meets our needs and has done so for me on many, many occasions.

I promise that these stories of provisions are true and that they did happen to me. There was a time after divorce when I needed money to fix my car and God sent two people to my home. One had an envelope in their hand and handed it to me with the comment, "God told us to give this to you." In the envelope was the exact amount of money for the car repair.

Another time, the heat pump in our home went out. A precious, obedient, generous person gave us $2,500 to meet that need. My husband had lost his job and had some health problems. During that time, we needed money to pay our bills. A woman in my Bible study gave me a check for $750, which helped to pay a lot of bills. Jeff opened his Bible a few days later and found $50. That was an encouragement he sorely needed that day. He jokingly commented that it sure does pay to read the Bible.

Another couple loaned us their camper and campsite so that we could have a vacation with our children. On another day, when I was working as a salesperson in a furniture store, I was having a very bad day. Another person in sales took credit for a sale I had made. He stole my commission, and this was not the first time. I was upset that Jeff was really sick at home. I prayed to God and told him that I needed to know that **He** really cared for me.

Not long after, a customer came in and asked me to go to his car with him, his wife, and his children. He told me that I might not understand but God told him to give me the

$20 bill that was in his glove box. That let me know that God cared and saw how I was treated unfairly. A week later, another customer wrote in about the other sales representative taking my commission and insisted that it be given to me. God does see all and care about everything.

On the day I received $20 from a customer, I had not yet eaten. I was permitted to be the first to leave work, so I stopped at a Chinese restaurant I had wanted to try. I ordered my favorite cashew chicken and debated if I should splurge on the crab Rangoon. I ordered both and thoroughly enjoyed the meal. As I asked for my ticket, my waitress told me that another customer paid my bill in order to celebrate her engagement that had happened that day. Wow! Isn't God good and all-knowing? I should say so. Praise God for his blessings.

"your Father knows what you need before you ask him."
—Matthew 6:8 (NIV)

My dad showed up at my office one day and asked for my car keys. He came back with new tires on my car. He said that he didn't want me driving around those "youngins" in a car with bald tires.

Another time, Dad came to our home with a brand-new riding mower because Jeff had been hospitalized with COPD and I was in the middle of chronic arthritis pain. My earthly father did this, so we can expect even more of this from our heavenly Father. God knows your need and already has the answer on its way.

Dear God,

I have needs but I realize that you already know this. Give me the faith and wisdom to know and trust that the answer is already on its way. Let me know you as my provider. Amen.

JEALOUS, WHO, ME?

"Love is patient, love is kind. Love is not jealous. It does not envy it does not boast, it is not proud. It does not dishonor others, it is not self-seeking, it is not easily angered, it keeps no record of wrongs. Love is not rude, is not selfish, and does not get upset. Love does not count up wrongs that have been done. Love does not delight in evil but rejoices with the truth. It always protects, always trusts, always hopes, always perseveres."

—1 Corinthians 13:4–7 (NIV)

When Jeff and I were engaged to be married, he went on a business trip and had not called me. I didn't know the hotel where he was staying. It was a time before cell phones, so I could not call him. I was so jealous that my mind conjured up a possibility.

I thought that he had met a flight attendant and was with her. We had only been engaged for a few months. I hadn't known him that long. Maybe he was the cheating type. I felt that I had a right to be jealous because I had been betrayed in the past.

I tossed and turned in my bed and allowed myself to be tormented. I remembered the scripture about love not being jealous. It does not mistrust. I was not doing that. I was missing the mark and not overcoming the obstacle before me. I said, *"Lord, I cannot live like this. Please deliver me from jealousy. Deliver me from not trusting Jeff."* Instantly, I felt peace. God started to give me the words to our wedding song. I got my pen and wrote them down. I felt such relief that I was able to fall asleep.

The next morning, Jeff called me. He apologized for not calling. He had carried his luggage in and hung up his business suits. Jeff laid down and fell asleep in his clothing. He did not awaken until the next morning.

Later that week, I told him about the incident. I showed him the words that God gave us for a wedding song. I asked if he thought he could put music to it. He said I think I already have it. He pulled out his guitar and played a tune that God had given him before the lyrics were written, They were perfect together. Thus, our song, **"God Gave Me You,"** was born in 1987. Our friend, Julie, who introduced us, sang the song at our wedding. Two of my good friends also used it for their wedding song. I would like to share the lyrics with you now.

God Gave Me You

Verse 1

I was so sad and lonely that I often prayed this prayer.
I need someone to hold me, Lord, someone to listen and to care.
Of course, he has to love me, God, but not as much as he loves you.
Then I'll be able to trust in him because he serves my Lord, too.
CHORUS
God gave me you. You took me in... just as I was, just as I am.
He gave me you...my brother, my friend,
to share my life with forever...without end.

Verse 2

Don't forget my children, Lord, he has to love them as his own.
So that he and I together can provide for them a home.
I prayed this over and over, wondering if it'd ever come true.
But, oh, I am so thankful, Jeff, that God gave me you.
REPEAT CHORUS...

Verse 3

I'm no longer sad and lonely because I prayed a simple prayer.
I now have you to hold me, to listen and to care.
The three of us can feel your love as it grows in every way.
How I give thanks to God above, for this...our wedding day.
REPEAT CHORUS

MARRIAGE TAKES THREE

"And if one can overpower him who is alone, two can resist him. A cord of three strands is not quickly torn apart."
—Ecclesiastes 4:12 (NASB)

One subject that is dear to my heart is marriage. I never considered divorce when I said my marriage vows, but it happened to me. The same thing happened to my sister after almost thirty-nine years of marriage. We know why God hates divorce. We saw the hurt it caused our children, just as God did.

After getting a divorce, I read and studied every book on marriage that I could find. I wanted to find out what happened and to make sure divorce never happened to me again.

When I remarried, I made sure that he was a Christian and that Jeff would love my children as his own. Jeff and I have been married for over thirty-four years. No, it was not always easy or perfect. The following is our story of making marriage work.

First and foremost, we each put God first in our marriage. That threefold cord is God, Jeff, and me. God taught us how to truly love one another and our children. As we went through trials, we trusted God to deliver us from sin and from ourselves. If I were to draw a triangle, I would put God at the top of the triangle. Jeff and I would be at the two bottom corners. God is the glue in a marriage. He holds it all together *if* we let Him.

We took every marriage class that we could. We went to marriage encounter and many couple's retreats. At each of those places, our marriage vows were repeated. Each time we said our marriage vows, it reminded us of what we had promised to one another and our Lord. If we needed to go to counseling, we did. We got over our pride and wanted to do what is right.

Can you let go of your pride and be willing to do any of the above things? The harder you work at something, and the more time you have invested, the better your marriage will be. "*Take note of this: everyone should be quick to listen, slow to speak and slow to become angry*" (James 1:19 (NIV)). Be the first one to say you are sorry. Fill up your minds with the Word of God and do your best to live out the Word. If possible, do a devotional together daily and pray together with one another and your children.

Are you having problems in your marriage? Are you about to give up on it?

Are you willing to work on it and try some of these suggestions? Can you put your marriage in His hands? Do you know another marriage in trouble? Are you willing to pray for that marriage? Pray with me.

Dear Jesus,

I surrender my marriage to you, my spouse to you, and my children to you. Help our family get better so that our home can glorify you. We don't want to become another statistic. Help our friends' marriages to become stronger too. Lord, teach me how to love like you love and always put my spouse and children before my job, my ministry, and myself. Show me what I can change in order to better my home. Amen.

Every marriage should begin in the presence of God.
Every child should be born in the presence of God.
We don't get married or have a child
and then go looking for God's presence.
—Pastor James Henson

Twelve Rules for a Happy Marriage

1. Never go to bed angry. It gives the devil more power in your marriage.
2. Never both be angry at once.
3. Yield to the wishes of your spouse as an exercise of self-discipline if for no other reason.
4. Never yell at one another unless the house is on fire.

5. If you have a choice to make your spouse look good or yourself look good, always choose to make your spouse look good.

6. Go out on a date once weekly if possible. Try to behave like the spouse your mate fell in love with. If you can't do it weekly, do it once a month and be romantic. Hold hands. Try a picnic. Men, bring her flowers. Open doors for her. Let her go first. Pull out her chair to seat her.

7. If you feel you must criticize, do so lovingly.

8. Neglect the whole world rather than your spouse.

9. Never allow your mate to come home without an affectionate welcome.

10. As soon as you realize you have made a mistake, ask sincerely for forgiveness.

11. Remember that it takes two to argue, the one who is wrong and the one who will be doing most of the talking.

12. A happy wife makes a happy life, so remember: the wife is always right.

LOVE IS AN ACTION VERB

"Dear friends, let us love one another, for love comes from God. Everyone who loves is born of God and knows God. Whoever does not love does not know God, because God is love."

—John 4:7–8 (NIV)

Love is not just a feeling; it is also an action verb. If you know God, then you are going to act like God. God loved most when He died for our sins. He loves by listening to us, answering prayers, meeting our needs, giving us grace, being our lawyer and defender, restoring lost years, speaking to us in a still, small voice, and sacrificing all for us.

I met a couple at a marriage retreat who I will never forget. He was a paraplegic in a wheelchair. She was really cute with a look of love in her eyes. They had fallen in love before the accident that crippled him. She loved him by living out her marriage vows, dressing him every morning, making sure he ate, putting him into the wheelchair, and believing in him. She supported him in whatever he did.

He had a beautiful voice and praised God in song. Besides his neck and head, he could only move one finger. He used it to dance before the Lord in his wheelchair. He could even pull wheelies in that wheelchair. He openly praised God for his wife. He joked that he knew when his wife was upset with him because she put his shirt on backwards.

His wife showed her love by serving her husband and by the sacrifices she made. Jesus showed his love by being a servant and sacrificing himself for us. How willing are we to make sacrifices for or to serve our mate? How willing are we to put our love into action? Sure, we can feel the emotion of love. That feeling will not always be present. That is why we put our love into action. By doing this, the feeling may even return.

How can we put our love into action for a neighbor, a friend, or a spouse? Can you take time to bake cookies for a neighbor? Can you send a card to encourage a friend? Could you make morning coffee for your spouse and leave a loving note with it?

Can you take the time to pray for your mate before they leave in the morning? Can you call a lonely friend and offer to take them to lunch? (Just make sure that the friend is of the same sex.) Are you willing to send money to someone in need?

You may already be doing this, or you may need to work on putting your love into action. No matter how we are doing, we can always do better. The Bible says that it is more blessed to give than to receive. By putting our love into action, we are giving of ourselves, our time, and the talents and gifts that God placed within us.

Dear Lord,

Help me to love like you love. Help me to show that love to others by putting it into action. Help me to be sensitive to others and know how I can bless them. Help me change my love into an action verb. Amen.

A PROPHETIC WORD

"But those who prophesy are speaking to people to give them strength, encouragement, and comfort."
—I Corinthians 14:3 (NCV) (According to Wikipedia, Biblical prophesy includes words that are given to humans or prophets as a communication from God to man.)

My husband and I have been given many words in the past that have come true sometime in the future. These words were encouraging. For example, many years ago, my husband and I were told that we would write songs together, and we have. Jeff was told through a prophetic word that he was blessed with the anointing of a worshiper through his instruments and songs and that he would play before thousands.

He has played before thousands when you count all the churches, home Bible studies, retreats, events, and other gatherings. We originally thought it was all at one time; however, that has not been the case yet. God has either answered it that way or plans to do so in the future.

I was told that my way of worship was through the written word. Many times in our church worship service, God would give me poetry to write and share with others. This is the way that He would give me prophetic words for the church body. I was also told that I would write books. This is thirty years later, but it is now happening.

God often communicates prophetic words to me to encourage others or to pray diligently for them. For example, he lets me know when marriages are in trouble. I would often tell my husband about marital problems that other couples were having. I would find out in the future that they had gotten a divorce. Finally, I discovered that so-called feeling about them was a prophetic word instead.

I say all of that to share that another prophetic word said that Jeff and I would be financially blessed. We always struggled to pay our bills because of financial emergencies such as hospital bills; however, God always made sure the bills were paid. When we receive a word, we just put it on a shelf and wait to see if it comes true. If not, it could be a false prophet.

This last year, Jeff's mother died. She had always lived a frugal lifestyle. His mom even used paper plates twice, so we didn't expect her inheritance to be as much as it was. Jeff and his sister, Cathy, were surprised when it was a significant amount of money. This is the way that the prophetic word that we would be blessed financially came to pass many years later.

I was finally able to purchase whatever I wanted to get at the grocery store instead of worrying about how much I was spending. We were able to do some home repairs. My husband was able to fulfill one of his dreams. Most of all, we are finally able to support two of our favorite charities and to help others.

Giving to others and encouraging them is what I love to do. Once when a dear friend of ours was going through divorce, I felt that we should give her some money to help out. When Jeff and I prayed about it, we agreed on the same amount to give to her. She was so appreciative and told us that she was down to her last $30. We were so happy that we heard from God and obeyed.

Jeff was always worried about dying and leaving only medical bills to me. He said that he is now so relieved that is not the case. Now, we can occasionally do something nice for our children and grandson. We are able to take our grandson, Ryder, on vacation with us to Gulf Shores, Alabama.

Has anybody ever spoken a prophetic word over you? Do you even believe that there are prophets today who can be used to bless you? Pray with me.

Lord Jesus,

Help me believe the word of God and that there are several prophetic words that came true throughout the Bible. Help me believe that there are prophets used in our day and age. If any words are spoken to me, let me put them on a shelf and wait for you to bring them to pass. Help me to believe and get renewed hope. Amen.

HAVE YOU SEEN AN ANGEL?

"Be not forgetful to entertain strangers: for thereby some have entertained angels unaware."
—Hebrews 13:2 (KJV)

An angel is a messenger of God to communicate with a man or woman.

There were several angels mentioned in the Bible. There is Michael, the Archangel. The Bible also talks about two men in shining garments who were in the tomb of Jesus when his mother, Mary Magdalene, and some other women went to put spices on Jesus' body. The stone was rolled away in the tomb and the body of Jesus was gone. Those angelic beings told the ladies that he was not there and that he had been raised from the dead.

169

Also, Jacob wrestled with an angel of God. The thirty-second chapter of Genesis says, "*Jacob went on his way and the angels of God met him*" (Genesis 32:1 (ASV)). Since the word of God is true, there are such things as angels. You have probably already met one.

I believe I met an angel when I had my stillborn baby girl. When the nurse walked into my room, a peace enveloped me. She ministered to me by caring for me and bringing comfort. When I asked for her the next morning, the other nurses said they didn't know any nurses who fit that description. She was the angel God sent to bring me comfort and peace.

In April of 1974, our area was hit by a series of tornadoes. Lives were lost. Land and trees were destroyed. Homes were lost. Some dear friends who rode my school bus could not make it home because of downed electric lines and debris in the road. When we finally made it to the house about an hour later, their home was flattened. Their mother was always home, so they feared that she might be dead.

What they did not know is that a stranger pulled into the driveway and blew the horn until she came out. This lady told her that a tornado was coming and that she needed to run to her cellar. The tornado nearly sucked her up before she could get in the cellar. She turned to look at the lady in the car, but both were gone. It is believed that God sent an angel to save her life. Having been there and seen the flattened home, I know that it was an angel of God who saved her.

Once Pastor James was praying for a dear friend who was very ill. His friend was in a hospital that was not very close in distance. As our church was praying, one of the ladies saw a large angel by his bedside in a vision. When Pastor made it to the hospital, the man's wife said her husband was touched at the time of our prayers and was doing much better. Besides the supernatural healing, the other thing that happened was the feather that was found on his pillow. An angel of God had visited him to bring healing and to steal him from the brink of death.

These angelic happenings are true. They are for today. Jesus sends them to us when we need encouragement, healing, or deliverance at a time that we really need the help of a heavenly being. How does that make you feel? A heavenly being is sent from heaven to earth just to minister to us. Isn't it awesome that God loves us that much?

Dear God,

Help me to believe that heavenly angels are real. They watch over me and I am not even aware of their presence. Deliver me of unbelief and teach me more about angels. Thank you for loving me so much and caring about me. Amen.

A WORD FROM THE LORD

"And it will come about after this that I will pour out my Spirit on all mankind; and your sons and daughters will prophesy, your old men will dream dreams, your young men will see visions."
—Joel 2:28 (NASB)

T he first time I met Tess was when my daughter was living with her dad. I was young and in such a bad state of mind that one of my friends invited me to a women's service. They said a lady named Tess would be the speaker. She was a pastor, a counselor, and a very learned woman of the things of God; she was also used in the gift of prophesy.

She was giving such beautiful, encouraging words of the Lord that it excited me to think of what she might say to me.

Trust me, it was not at all like I had imagined. Tess said to me, "I am about to give you a word that God has not given me before. He said to my spirit that you are called to adversity, but people watch you. They watch how you respond to the adversity that comes your way. Because of this, you will literally yank some from the pits of hell."

I was not only unhappy, but I did not think the word was from God.

I decided to myself that she must be a false prophet. I asked God to show me the truth, though.

As I was driving down the road the next morning and turned on the radio, I heard a sermon about adversity. I picked up my devotional and it was about adversity. I picked up a Charles Stanley book that a friend gave to me. When I turned the page, the next chapter was about adversity. I said, "Okay, Lord, I hear you."

I began to study adversity and what advantages come from it. First and foremost, it brings us closer to God if we allow it to do so. It pushes us to get into the word of God. Adversity purifies us as gold. It teaches us to overcome. It gives us a testimony and encourages others as we share our testimony.

This is not the road I would have chosen, but evidently, this was God's plan for me. I often referred to myself as Jobette because I went through so many trials. God always brought me through to the other side, though. He always gave me another testimony.

This book was born out of those trials. This book was born out of those testimonies. Since the Lord always took care of me, my testimony can encourage you as you read this book. If it has helped, pass it on to a friend or buy a copy to give to a hurting friend. Our Lord is a deliverer, a healer, a friend who sticks closer to us than a brother, is with us **always**, and is an all-knowing God.

Dear Lord,

Teach me that adversity is not always bad. Teach me not to complain. Encourage me and give me new hope. Help me to overcome. Help me to encourage others. Put joy in my heart so that I can be a good example of one whose God will go through the trial with me. Amen.

IN SUMMARY

1. *"Hope deferred makes the heart sick but a longing fulfilled is a tree of life."* ~ *Proverbs 13:12 (NIV) (You must **never give up hope**. If you have, get it back by reading and memorizing the word of God!)*
2. *"...Put your hope in God, for I will yet praise him, my Savior and my God."* ~ *Psalms 42:11 (NIV)*
3. *"Through him you believed in God, who raised him from the dead and glorified him, and so your faith and hope are in God."* ~ *I Peter 1:21 (NIV)*
4. *"Everyone who puts this hope in him purifies himself, just as he is pure."* ~ *I John 3:3 (NIV)*
5. *"which is Christ in you, the hope of glory."* ~ *Colossians 1:27 (NIV)*

6. *"Be strong and take heart all you who hope in the Lord."*
   ~ Psalms 31:24 (NIV)

7. *"For you have been my hope, O Sovereign Lord, confidence since my youth." ~ Psalms 71:5 (NIV)*

8. *"Be on your guard; stand firm in the faith; be of good courage; stand strong." I Corinthians 16:13 (NIV)*

9. *"So faith comes from hearing, and hearing through the word of Christ." ~ Romans 10:17 (NIV)*

10. *"Now faith is being sure of what we hope for and certain of what we do not see." ~ Hebrews 11:1 (NIV)*

Read and memorize the above scriptures so that God can bring them to your remembrance when you need them. Our mind is like a computer in the way that you cannot access something that has never been put into it. Write your favorite verses on your mirror, your refrigerator, and your desk—or whatever works best for you.

I remember a magnet on my mom's refrigerator when I was just beginning my public speaking and preaching. It said, "Lord, fill my mouth with worthwhile stuff, and nudge me when I've said enough." I used to end my opening prayer before speaking or teaching with this phrase.

Fellowship with friends of faith who can encourage you. Find a good church. Recognize and bind the mindset of Satan. Listen to Christian music to build up your most holy faith. Start your day with scripture.

Remember that God is good. He sent Jesus to die for you because he loves you so much. He is on your side. He is not willing that anyone should perish, so he provided a way for you to escape hell. He always has the answer if you seek him. Nothing is too difficult for our God. Most of all, Jesus loves you, loves you, loves you!

I hope that you have enjoyed reading this book as much as I have enjoyed hearing from the Lord and writing it. If so, or if you know somebody it can bless, pass on the hope.

May God bless you richly and continue to draw you close to him. I pray that God uses this book to change your life and those whose lives you touch. May this book continue to minister, even after God calls me to my heavenly home. Blessed be the name of the Lord, our God!

ABOUT THE AUTHOR

Cheryl Diane Meyer likes to be called Diane because that is what her family and friends have always called her. Diane has always lived in Southern Indiana. While in Chicago, she was called a Southern Belle because of her southern accent. Diane and her husband live in Depauw, Indiana. They have been married for over thirty-four years and have two grown children and a grandson who they cherish.

Diane is a published poet and has been published in a magazine from The School Meals Advisory Council. She was published in a book called *A Showcase of Poets* with her poem highlighted on the first page of the book. Diane loves to write and has been doing so since the second grade when the teacher read her story to the class because it was her favorite. This is her first book but will not be her last.

A free ebook edition is available with the purchase of this book.

To claim your free ebook edition:

Visit MorganJamesBOGO.com
Sign your name CLEARLY in the space
Complete the form and submit a photo of
the entire copyright page
You or your friend can download the ebook
to your preferred device

Morgan James
BOGO™

A **FREE** ebook edition is available for you
or a friend with the purchase of this print book.

CLEARLY SIGN YOUR NAME ABOVE

Instructions to claim your free ebook edition:
1. Visit MorganJamesBOGO.com
2. Sign your name CLEARLY in the space above
3. Complete the form and submit a photo
   of this entire page
4. You or your friend can download the ebook
   to your preferred device

Print & Digital Together Forever.

Snap a photo   Free ebook   Read anywhere

CPSIA information can be obtained
at www.ICGtesting.com
Printed in the USA
JSHW050149020622
26614JS00001B/21

9 781631 957611